everyday
vegetarian

Bath · New York · Singapore · Hong Kong · Cologne · Delhi · Melbourne

This edition published by Parragon in 2009

Parragon
Queen Street House
4 Queen Street
Bath BA1 1HE, UK

ISBN 978-1-4054-9399-4

Printed in China

This book uses metric and imperial measurements. Follow the same units of measurement throughout; do not mix metric and imperial. All spoon measurements are level, unless otherwise stated: teaspoons are assumed to be 5ml, and tablespoons are assumed to be 15ml. Unless otherwise stated, milk is assumed to be whole, eggs and individual fruits such as bananas are medium, and pepper is freshly ground black pepper.

Recipes using raw or very lightly cooked eggs should be avoided by infants, the elderly, pregnant women, convalescents, and anyone suffering from an illness. Pregnant and breast-feeding women are advised to avoid eating peanuts and peanut products.

everyday
vegetarian

introduction

Following a vegetarian diet was once considered to be rather eccentric and certainly very dull! However, in recent years more and more people have chosen to embrace a meat-free diet, for a number of reasons. The most obvious of these is a desire not to eat animals or fish, but health issues often come into the equation too – for example, sufferers of irritable bowel syndrome often find that meat is one of the triggers for the symptoms. Meat and fish can also be expensive, so even non-vegetarians often choose to have two or three meat-free meals each week.

The really good news is that the ever-increasing interest in vegetarianism has raised its profile in the world of gastronomy. Chefs have risen to the challenge with skill and enthusiasm and have come up with some truly creative recipes – and the meat-free diet is no longer dull!

If you are new to vegetarianism, it is important to remember that you cannot simply exclude meat and fish from your usual recipes, because this will deprive you of protein and other vital nutrients that are essential to your  health and wellbeing. Meat and fish must be replaced with other protein- and nutrient-rich foods such as beans, nuts and seeds, tofu and dairy products. If you have allergies to any of these foods, take advice from your doctor or a nutritionist to ensure that you will not damage your health instead of enhancing it.

Whether you are planning to be a 'proper' vegetarian, or you are having vegetarian guests to dinner, or you just want to ring the changes and have an occasional meal without meat, there are

some fabulous ideas in this book, taken from around the world. For the best results, choose really fresh, top-quality ingredients – this will ensure that you get the maximum goodness out of your food, as well as superb flavour.

Have fun experimenting!

light meals & starters

Many of the world's favourite classic dishes are made with vegetables and there are some great recipes here for soups, dips and starters. Try a light and delicate Watercress Soup, a hearty White Bean Soup or the thick and satisfying Monk's Soup – there's no hint of austerity here, whatever the name might imply! Put together a Spanish tapas selection, such as Salted Almonds, Cracked Marinated Olives, Aubergine Dip, Sautéed Garlic Mushrooms and Figs with Blue Cheese, or do as the French do and start your meal with the Mixed Salad Selection – a refreshing combination of celeriac, carrot and beetroot that will really make your palate tingle.

Some of these recipes also make ideal light dishes. For brunch, lunch or a late-evening snack, try Courgette Fritters with Yogurt Dip, Cheese & Herb Soufflés with Sautéed Mushrooms, Sweet Potato, Mint & Feta Patties, or Stuffed Portabello Mushrooms. If you love Mexican-style food, go for Guacamole or Black Bean Nachos, and for a hint of the Middle East try Hummus Dip or Falafel with Tahini Sauce. There is enough nutrition in these dishes to keep you feeling satisfied for hours!

If, however, you just want the most perfect, simple, elegant starter, serve Asparagus with Melted Butter. Wonderful!

salted almonds

ingredients

SERVES 6–8

225 g/8 oz whole almonds, in
  their skins or blanched
  (see method)

4 tbsp Spanish olive oil

coarse sea salt

1 tsp paprika or ground
  cumin (optional)

method

1 Fresh almonds in their skins are superior in taste, but blanched almonds are much more convenient. If the almonds are not blanched, put them in a bowl, cover with boiling water for 3–4 minutes, then plunge them into cold water for 1 minute. Drain them well in a sieve, then slide off the skins between your fingers. Dry the almonds well on kitchen paper.

2 Put the olive oil in a roasting pan and swirl it round so that it covers the bottom. Add the almonds and toss them in the pan so that they are evenly coated in the oil, then spread them out in a single layer.

3 Roast the almonds in a preheated oven, 180°C/350°F/Gas Mark 4, for 20 minutes, or until they are light golden brown, tossing several times during the cooking. Drain the almonds on kitchen paper, then transfer them to a bowl.

4 While the almonds are still warm, sprinkle with plenty of sea salt and the paprika or cumin, if using, and toss well together to coat. Serve the almonds warm or cold. The almonds are at their best when served freshly cooked, so, if possible, cook them on the day that you plan to eat them. However, they can be stored in an airtight container for up to 3 days.

cracked marinated olives

ingredients

SERVES 8

450 g/1 lb can or jar unpitted
    large green olives, drained

4 garlic cloves, peeled

2 tsp coriander seeds

1 small lemon

4 sprigs of fresh thyme

4 feathery stalks of fennel

2 small fresh red chillies
    (optional)

pepper

Spanish extra-virgin olive oil,
    to cover

slices of fresh crusty bread,
    to serve

method

1 To allow the flavours of the marinade to penetrate the olives, place the olives on a cutting board and, using a rolling pin, bash them lightly so that they crack slightly. Alternatively, use a sharp knife to cut a lengthways slit in each olive as far as the stone. Using the flat side of a broad knife, lightly crush each garlic clove. Using a pestle and mortar, crack the coriander seeds. Cut the lemon, with its rind, into small chunks.

2 Put the olives, garlic, coriander seeds, lemon chunks, thyme sprigs, fennel and chillies, if using, in a large bowl and toss together. Season with pepper, but you should not need to add salt as preserved olives are usually salty enough. Pack the ingredients tightly into a glass jar with a lid. Pour in enough olive oil to cover the olives, then seal the jar tightly.

3 Let the olives stand at room temperature for 24 hours, then marinate in the refrigerator for at least 1 week but preferably 2 weeks before serving. From time to time, gently give the jar a shake to remix the ingredients. Return the olives to room temperature and remove from the oil to serve. Provide cocktail sticks for spearing the olives. Serve with slices of fresh crusty bread.

guacamole

ingredients

SERVES 4

2 large, ripe avocados

juice of 1 lime, or to taste

2 tsp olive oil

$1/2$ onion, finely chopped

1 fresh green chilli, such as
poblano, deseeded and
finely chopped

1 garlic clove, crushed

$1/4$ tsp ground cumin

1 tbsp chopped fresh
coriander, plus extra
leaves to garnish (optional)

salt and pepper

method

1 Cut the avocados in half lengthways and twist the 2 halves in opposite directions to separate. Stab the stone with the point of a sharp knife and lift out.

2 Peel, then coarsely chop, the avocado halves and place in a non-metallic bowl. Squeeze over the lime juice and add the oil.

3 Mash the avocados with a fork until the desired consistency is reached – either chunky or smooth. Blend in the onion, chilli, garlic, cumin and chopped coriander, then season with salt and pepper.

4 Transfer to a serving dish and serve at once, to avoid discoloration, garnished with the coriander leaves, if liked.

aubergine dip

ingredients

SERVES 6–8

olive oil

1 large aubergine,
    about 400 g/14 oz

2 spring onions, chopped
    finely

1 large garlic clove, crushed

2 tbsp finely chopped fresh
    parsley

salt and pepper

smoked sweet Spanish paprika,
    to garnish

French bread, to serve

method

1 Heat 4 tablespoons of oil in a large frying pan over medium–high heat. Add the aubergine slices and cook on both sides until soft and starting to brown. Remove from the pan and set aside to cool. The slices will release the oil again as they cool.

2 Heat another tablespoon of oil in the frying pan. Add the spring onions and garlic and cook for 3 minutes, or until the spring onions become soft. Remove from the heat and set aside with the aubergine slices to cool.

3 Transfer all the ingredients to a food processor and process just until a coarse purée forms. Transfer to a serving bowl and stir in the parsley. Taste and adjust the seasoning, if necessary. Serve at once, or cover and chill until 15 minutes before required. Sprinkle with paprika and serve with slices of French bread.

hummus

ingredients

SERVES 8

225 g/8 oz dried chickpeas,
    covered with water and
    soaked overnight
juice of 2 large lemons
150 ml/5 fl oz tahini
2 garlic cloves, crushed
4 tbsp extra-virgin olive oil
small pinch of ground cumin
salt and pepper
1 tsp paprika
chopped flat-leaf parsley,
    to garnish
pitta bread, to serve

method

1 Drain the chickpeas, put in a saucepan, and cover with cold water. Bring to the boil then let simmer for about 2 hours, until very tender.

2 Drain the chickpeas, reserving a little of the liquid, and put in a food processor, reserving a few to garnish. Blend the chickpeas until smooth, gradually adding the lemon juice and enough reserved liquid to form a smooth, thick purée.

3 Add the tahini, garlic, 3 tablespoons of the olive oil and the cumin and blend until smooth. Season with salt and pepper.

4 Turn the mixture into a shallow serving dish and chill in the refrigerator for 2–3 hours before serving.

5 To serve, mix the reserved olive oil with the paprika and drizzle over the top of the dish. Sprinkle with the parsley and the reserved chickpeas. Accompany with warm pitta bread.

vegetable soup with pesto

ingredients

SERVES 4

1 litre/32 fl oz fresh cold
    water
bouquet garni of 1 fresh parsley
    sprig, 1 fresh thyme sprig,
    and 1 bay leaf, tied together
    with clean string
2 celery stalks, chopped
3 baby leeks, chopped
4 baby carrots, chopped
150 g/5$^1/_2$ oz new potatoes,
    scrubbed and cut into
    bite-size chunks
4 tbsp shelled broad beans
    or peas
175 g/6 oz canned cannellini
    or flageolet beans, drained
    and rinsed
3 heads pak choi
150 g/5$^1/_2$ oz rocket
pepper

pesto

2 large handfuls fresh basil
    leaves
1 fresh green chilli, deseeded
2 garlic cloves
4 tbsp olive oil
1 tsp Parmesan cheese,
    finely grated

method

1 Put the water and bouquet garni into a
large saucepan and add the celery, leeks,
carrots and potatoes. Bring to the boil, then
reduce the heat and simmer for 10 minutes.

2 Stir in the broad beans or peas and canned
beans and simmer for a further 10 minutes.
Stir in the pak choi and rocket, season with
pepper and simmer for a further 2–3 minutes.
Remove and discard the bouquet garni.

3 Meanwhile, to make the pesto, put the basil,
chilli, garlic and oil into a food processor and
pulse to form a thick paste. Stir in the cheese.

4 Stir most of the pesto into the soup, then
ladle into warmed bowls. Top with the
remaining pesto and serve at once.

white bean soup

ingredients

SERVES 4

175 g/6 oz dried cannellini
  beans, soaked in cold
  water to cover overnight

1.5 litres/48 fl oz vegetable
  stock

115 g/4 oz dried corallini,
  conchigliette piccole,
  or other soup pasta

6 tbsp olive oil

2 garlic cloves, finely chopped

4 tbsp chopped fresh
  flat-leaf parsley

salt and pepper

fresh crusty bread, to serve

method

1 Drain the soaked beans and place them in a large, heavy-based saucepan. Add the stock and bring to the boil. Partially cover the pan, then reduce the heat and simmer for 2 hours, or until tender.

2 Transfer about half the beans and a little of the stock to a food processor or blender and process to a smooth purée. Return the purée to the pan and stir well to mix. Return the soup to the boil.

3 Add the pasta to the soup, return to the boil and cook for 10 minutes, or until tender.

4 Meanwhile, heat 4 tablespoons of the olive oil in a small saucepan. Add the garlic and cook over low heat, stirring frequently, for 4–5 minutes, or until golden. Stir the garlic into the soup and add the parsley. Season with salt and pepper and ladle into warmed soup bowls. Drizzle with the remaining olive oil and serve immediately with crusty bread.

watercress soup

ingredients

SERVES 4

2 bunches of watercress
    (approx 200 g/7 oz),
    thoroughly cleaned

3 tbsp butter

2 onions, chopped

225 g/8 oz potatoes, peeled
    and roughly chopped

1.25 litres/40 fl oz vegetable
    stock or water

salt and pepper

whole nutmeg, for grating
    (optional)

125 ml/4 fl oz crème fraîche,
    yogurt, or sour cream

method

1 Remove the leaves from the stalks of the watercress and keep on one side. Roughly chop the stalks.

2 Melt the butter in a large saucepan over medium heat, add the onion and cook for 4–5 minutes until soft. Do not brown.

3 Add the potato to the pan and mix well with the onion. Add the watercress stalks and the stock. Bring to the boil, then reduce the heat, cover and simmer for 15–20 minutes until the potato is soft.

4 Add the watercress leaves and stir in to heat through. Remove from the heat and use a hand-held stick blender to process the soup until smooth. Alternatively, pour the soup into a blender, process until smooth, and return to the rinsed-out pan. Reheat and season with salt and pepper, adding a good grating of nutmeg, if using.

5 Serve in warm bowls with the crème fraîche, yogurt or sour cream spooned on top.

borscht

ingredients

SERVES 6

1 onion

4 tbsp butter

350 g/12 oz raw beetroot, cut into thin sticks, and 1 raw beetroot, grated

1 carrot, cut into thin sticks

3 celery stalks, thinly sliced

2 tomatoes, peeled, deseeded and chopped

2 large fresh dill sprigs

1.5 litres/48 fl oz vegetable stock

1 tbsp white wine vinegar

1 tbsp sugar

salt and pepper

115 g/4 oz white cabbage, shredded

150 ml/5 fl oz sour cream, to garnish

method

1 Slice the onion into rings. Melt the butter in a large, heavy-based pan over low heat. Add the onion and cook, stirring frequently, for 5 minutes or until softened. Add the beetroot sticks, carrot, celery and tomatoes and cook, stirring frequently, for 4–5 minutes.

2 Snip one of the dill sprigs. Add the stock, vinegar, sugar and the snipped dill to the pan. Season with salt and pepper. Bring to the boil, then reduce the heat and simmer for 35–40 minutes until the vegetables are tender.

3 Stir in the cabbage, cover and simmer for a further 10 minutes. Stir in the grated beetroot, with any juices, and cook for a further 10 minutes. Ladle into warmed bowls. Garnish with a spoonful of sour cream and snip the remaining dill over the top.

monk's soup

ingredients

SERVES 4

1 litre/32 fl oz vegetable stock

1 stalk lemon grass, centre
part only, finely chopped

1 tsp tamarind paste

pinch of dried red pepper
flakes, or to taste

140 g/5 oz thin green beans,
cut into 2.5-cm/1-inch
pieces

1 tbsp light soy sauce

1 tsp brown sugar

juice of 1/2 lime

250 g/9 oz firm tofu, drained
and cut into small cubes

2 spring onions, sliced
diagonally

55 g/2 oz enoki mushrooms,
hard end of the stalks cut off

400 g/14 oz fresh udon noodles
or thick Chinese egg
noodles

method

1 Put the stock in a large pan with the lemon grass, tamarind paste and red pepper flakes and bring to the boil, stirring until the tamarind dissolves. Lower the heat, add the green beans and simmer for 6 minutes. Add the soy sauce, brown sugar and lime juice. Taste and stir in more sugar, lime juice or red pepper flakes if liked.

2 Stir in the tofu and spring onions and continue simmering for just 1–2 minutes longer, or until the green beans are tender, but still with a bit of bite, and the tofu is warm. Add the enoki mushrooms.

3 Pour boiling water over the udon noodles to separate them, then divide them between 4 large bowls and divide the soup between the bowls. The heat of the soup will warm the noodles.

chinese mushroom soup

ingredients

SERVES 4

15 g/$^{1}/_{2}$ oz dried Chinese
    wood ear mushrooms

115 g/4 oz dried thin Chinese
    egg noodles

2 tsp arrowroot or cornstarch

1 litre/32 fl oz vegetable stock

5-cm/2-inch piece fresh root
    ginger, peeled and sliced

2 tbsp dark soy sauce

2 tsp mirin or sweet sherry

1 tsp rice vinegar

4 small pak choi, each cut
    in half

salt and pepper

snipped fresh Chinese or
    ordinary chives, to garnish

method

1 Put the dried wood ear mushrooms in a heatproof bowl and pour over enough boiling water to cover, then let stand for 20 minutes, or until tender. Meanwhile, boil the noodles for 3 minutes, or according to the package instructions, until soft. Drain well and rinse with cold water to stop the noodles cooking, and set aside.

2 Strain the mushrooms through a sieve lined with a dish towel and reserve the liquid. Leave the mushrooms whole or slice them, depending on how large they are. Put the arrowroot in a wok or large pan and gradually stir in the reserved mushroom liquid. Add the vegetable stock, sliced ginger, soy sauce, mirin, rice vinegar, mushrooms and pak choi and bring to the boil, stirring constantly. Lower the heat and simmer for 15 minutes.

3 Add salt and pepper, but remember that soy sauce is salty so you might not need any salt at all – taste first. Use a slotted spoon to remove the pieces of ginger.

4 Divide the noodles between 4 bowls, then spoon the soup over and garnish with chives.

sautéed garlic mushrooms

ingredients

SERVES 6

450 g/1 lb white mushrooms

5 tbsp Spanish olive oil

2 garlic cloves, finely chopped

squeeze of lemon juice

salt and pepper

4 tbsp chopped fresh
    flat-leaf parsley

crusty bread, to serve

method

1 Wipe or brush clean the mushrooms, then trim off the stalks close to the caps. Cut any large mushrooms in half or into quarters. Heat the olive oil in a large, heavy-based frying pan, add the garlic and cook for 30 seconds–1 minute, or until lightly browned. Add the mushrooms and sauté over high heat, stirring most of the time, until the mushrooms have absorbed all the oil in the pan.

2 Reduce the heat to low. When the juices have come out of the mushrooms, increase the heat again, and sauté for 4–5 minutes, stirring most of the time, until the juices have almost evaporated. Add a squeeze of lemon juice and season to taste with salt and pepper. Stir in the chopped parsley and cook for a further minute.

3 Transfer the sautéed mushrooms to a warmed serving dish and serve piping hot or warm. Accompany with chunks or slices of crusty bread for mopping up the garlic cooking juices.

mixed salad selection

ingredients

SERVES 4–6

celeriac rémoulade

1 large egg yolk
1 tbsp Dijon mustard
^{1}/$_2$ tsp red wine vinegar
150 ml/5 fl oz sunflower oil
salt and pepper
1^1/$_2$ tsp lemon juice
1 tsp salt
450 g/1 lb celeriac

carrot salad

450 g/1 lb carrots, peeled
2 tbsp olive oil
2 tbsp freshly squeezed
    orange juice
salt and pepper
2 tbsp finely chopped
    almonds
1 tbsp finely chopped fresh
    flat-leaf parsley

beetroot salad

400 g/14 oz cooked beetroot,
    peeled
2 tbsp vinaigrette
1 tbsp snipped fresh chives

slices of French bread and
    unsalted butter, to serve

method

1 To make the rémoulade sauce, whiz the egg yolk, mustard and red wine vinegar in a food processor or blender until blended. With the motor still running, pour the oil through the feed tube, drop by drop, until the sauce starts to thicken, then add the remainder of the oil in a slow, steady stream. Season to taste with salt and pepper.

2 Put the lemon juice and salt in a large bowl of water. Finely shred the celeriac into the acidulated water to prevent discoloration. Drain and pat dry, then stir into the rémoulade sauce. Let stand for 20 minutes at room temperature before serving.

3 To make the carrot salad, finely shred the carrots into a bowl with the olive oil and orange juice and toss together. Season with salt and pepper and cover and chill until required. Stir in the almonds and parsley just before serving.

4 To make the beetroot salad, cut the beetroot into 5-mm/^{1}/$_4$-inch dice. Put the diced beetroot in a bowl, then add the vinaigrette and toss together. Cover and chill until required. Stir in the chives just before serving.

5 To serve, divide the celeriac rémoulade, carrot salad and beetroot salad between individual plates and accompany with plenty of French bread and butter.

figs with blue cheese

ingredients

SERVES 6

caramelized
almonds

100 g/3¹/₂ oz caster sugar

115 g/4 oz whole almonds,
    blanched or unblanched

12 ripe figs

350 g/12 oz Spanish blue
    cheese, such as Picós,
    crumbled

extra-virgin olive oil

method

1 First make the caramelized almonds. Put the sugar in a saucepan over medium–high heat and stir until the sugar melts, turns golden brown and bubbles: do not stir once the mixture starts to bubble. Remove from the heat and add the almonds one at a time and quickly turn with a fork until coated; if the caramel hardens, return the pan to the heat. Transfer each almond to a lightly buttered baking sheet once it is coated. Let stand until cool and firm.

2 To serve, slice the figs in half and arrange 4 halves on each plate. Coarsely chop the almonds by hand, reserving a few whole ones for garnish. Place a mound of blue cheese on each plate and sprinkle with chopped almonds. Drizzle the figs very lightly with the oil and garnish with the reserved, whole almonds.

asparagus with melted butter

ingredients

SERVES 2

16–20 stalks of asparagus, trimmed to about 20 cm/8 inches

85 g/3 oz unsalted butter, melted

sea salt and pepper, to serve

method

1 Remove some of the base of the asparagus stalks with a potato peeler if they are rather thick. Tie the stalks together with string or use a wire basket so that they can easily be removed from the saucepan without damage.

2 Bring a large saucepan of salted water to the boil and plunge in the stalks. Cover with a lid and cook for 4–5 minutes. Pierce one stalk near the base with a sharp knife. If it is fairly soft remove from the heat at once. Do not overcook asparagus or the tender tips will fall off.

3 Drain the asparagus thoroughly and serve on large warmed plates with the butter poured over. Both the butter and the asparagus should be warm rather than hot. Serve with sea salt and pepper for sprinkling.

courgette fritters with yogurt dip

ingredients

SERVES 4

2–3 courgettes, about 400 g/
    14 oz
1 garlic clove, crushed
3 spring onions, finely sliced
125 g/4¹/₂ oz feta cheese,
    crumbled
2 tbsp finely chopped
    fresh parsley
2 tbsp finely chopped
    fresh mint
1 tbsp finely chopped fresh dill
¹/₂ tsp freshly grated nutmeg
2 tbsp all-purpose flour
pepper
2 eggs
2 tbsp olive oil
1 lemon, cut into quarters,
    to garnish

yogurt dip
250 g/9 oz strained plain
    yogurt
¹/₄ cucumber, diced
1 tbsp finely chopped fresh dill
pepper

method

1 Grate the courgettes straight onto a clean tea towel and cover with another. Pat well and set aside for 10 minutes until the courgettes are dry.

2 Meanwhile, to make the dip, mix the yogurt, cucumber, dill and pepper in a serving bowl. Cover and chill.

3 Tip the courgettes into a large mixing bowl. Stir in the garlic, spring onions, cheese, herbs, nutmeg, flour and pepper. Beat the eggs in a separate bowl and stir into the courgette mixture – the batter will be quite lumpy and uneven but this is fine.

4 Heat the oil in a large, wide frying pan over medium heat. Drop 4 tablespoonfuls of the batter into the pan, with space in between, and cook for 2–3 minutes on each side. Remove, drain on kitchen paper and keep warm. Cook the second batch of fritters in the same way. (There should be 8 fritters in total.)

5 Serve the fritters hot with the dip, garnished with lemon quarters.

cheese & herb soufflés with sautéed mushrooms

ingredients

MAKES 6 SOUFFLÉS

55 g/2 oz butter, plus extra, melted, for greasing

40 g/1^1/$_2$ oz all-purpose flour

150 ml/5 fl oz milk

250 g/9 oz ricotta cheese

4 eggs, separated, plus 2 egg whites

2 tbsp finely chopped fresh parsley

2 tbsp finely chopped fresh thyme

1 tbsp finely chopped fresh rosemary

salt and pepper

200 ml/7 fl oz light cream

6 tbsp grated Parmesan cheese

sautéed white mushrooms, to serve

method

1 Brush 6 x 9-cm/3^1/$_2$-inch soufflé dishes well with melted butter and set aside. Melt the butter in a medium pan, add the flour and cook for 30 seconds, stirring constantly. Whisk in the milk and continue whisking over low heat until the mixture thickens. Cook for a further 30 seconds. Remove from the heat and beat in the ricotta. Add the egg yolks and herbs and season well with salt and pepper.

2 Beat the egg whites in a clean bowl until they form stiff peaks and gently fold them through the ricotta mixture. Spoon into the prepared dishes, filling them just to the top. Place in a baking dish and pour in enough boiling water to come halfway up the sides of the dishes. Bake the soufflés in a preheated oven, 180°C/350°F/Gas Mark 4, for 15–20 minutes, or until well risen and browned. Remove from the oven, cool for 10 minutes, then gently ease out of their moulds. Place in a lightly greased ovenproof dish and cover with clingfilm.

3 Increase the oven temperature to 200°C/400°F/Gas Mark 6. Remove the clingfilm and pour the cream evenly over the soufflés, sprinkle with Parmesan and return to the oven for a further 15 minutes. Serve at once with sautéed mushrooms.

artichokes with vièrge sauce

ingredients

SERVES 4

4 large globe artichokes

$^1/_2$ lemon, sliced

salt

vièrge sauce

3 large beefsteak tomatoes, peeled and deseeded, then finely diced

4 spring onions, very finely chopped

6 tbsp chopped fresh herbs, such as basil, chervil, chives, mint, flat-leaf parsley, or tarragon

150 ml/5 fl oz full-flavoured extra-virgin olive oil

pinch of sugar

salt and pepper

method

1 To prepare the artichokes, cut off the stems and trim the bottom so that they will stand upright on the plate. Use scissors to snip the leaf tips off each one, then drop in a large bowl of water with 2 of the lemon slices while the others are being prepared.

2 Select a saucepan large enough to hold the 4 artichokes upright and half-fill with salted water and the remaining lemon slices. Bring the water to the boil, then add the artichokes and place a heatproof plate on top to keep them submerged. Reduce the heat to a low boil and continue boiling the artichokes for 25–35 minutes, depending on their size, until the bottom leaves pull out easily.

3 While the artichokes are cooking, prepare the vièrge sauce. Put the tomatoes, spring onions, herbs, oil, sugar and salt and pepper to taste in a saucepan and set aside for the flavours to blend.

4 When the artichokes are tender, drain them upside-down on kitchen paper, then transfer to individual plates. Heat the sauce very gently until it is just warm, then spoon it equally over the artichokes to serve.

sweet potato, mint & feta patties

ingredients

SERVES 4

600 g/1 lb 5 oz sweet potatoes,
    peeled and grated
1 egg, lightly beaten
50 g/1³/4 oz all-purpose flour
70 g/2¹/2 oz butter, melted
100 g/3¹/2 oz feta cheese,
    crumbled
3 tbsp chopped fresh mint
salt and pepper
1 tbsp vegetable oil
4 tbsp sour cream
2 tbsp chopped fresh parsley,
    to garnish

method

1 Mix the grated sweet potato with the egg, flour, melted butter, feta and mint until well combined. Season the mixture to taste with salt and pepper.

2 Heat the oil in a large non-stick frying pan over medium heat. Spoon large tablespoons of the mixture into patties, flattening slightly, and cook on both sides in batches until golden brown.

3 Slide the patties onto a baking sheet covered with parchment paper and bake in a preheated oven, 160°C/325°F/Gas Mark 2¹/2, for 15 minutes, or until crisp. Place 2 patties on each plate, top with a tablespoon of sour cream and garnish with a little chopped parsley. Serve at once.

stuffed portobello mushrooms

ingredients

SERVES 4

12 large portobello mushrooms, wiped over and stems removed

2 tbsp corn oil, plus extra for oiling

1 fennel bulb, stalks removed, finely chopped

100 g/3^1/$_2$ oz sun-dried tomatoes, finely chopped

2 garlic cloves, crushed

125 g/4^1/$_2$ oz grated fontina cheese

50 g/1^3/$_4$ oz freshly grated Parmesan cheese

3 tbsp chopped fresh basil

salt and pepper

1 tbsp olive oil

fresh Parmesan cheese shavings

1 tbsp chopped fresh parsley, to serve

method

1 Place 8 of the mushrooms, cup-side up, in a large, lightly oiled ovenproof dish and chop the remaining 4 mushrooms finely.

2 Heat the corn oil in a non-stick frying pan, add the chopped mushrooms, fennel, sun-dried tomatoes and garlic and cook over low heat until the vegetables are soft, but not browned. Remove from the heat and let cool.

3 When cool, add the cheeses, basil, salt and pepper. Mix well. Brush the mushrooms lightly with the olive oil and fill each cavity with a spoonful of the vegetable filling. Bake in a preheated oven, 180°C/350°F/Gas Mark 4, for 20–25 minutes, or until the mushrooms are tender and the filling is heated through.

4 Top with Parmesan shavings and parsley and serve at once, allowing 2 mushrooms for each person.

falafel with tahini sauce

ingredients

SERVES 4

450 g/1 lb canned cannellini
    beans, drained

350 g/12 oz canned
    chickpeas, drained

1 onion, finely chopped

2 garlic cloves, chopped

1 small fresh red chilli,
    deseeded and chopped

1 tsp baking powder

25 g/1 oz fresh parsley,
    chopped, plus extra
    sprigs to garnish

pinch of cayenne

2 tbsp water

salt and pepper

vegetable oil, for deep-frying

pitta bread, thick plain yogurt
    or yogurt dip (see page
    38), and lemon wedges,
    to serve

tahini sauce

200 ml/7 fl oz tahini

1 garlic clove, chopped

1–2 tbsp water

2–3 tsp lemon juice, to taste

method

1 To make the tahini sauce, put the tahini and garlic in a bowl. Gradually stir in the water until a fairly smooth consistency is reached, then stir in the lemon juice. Add more water or lemon juice, if necessary. Cover with clingfilm and chill in the refrigerator until required.

2 To make the falafel, rinse and drain the beans and chickpeas. Put them in a food processor with the onion, garlic, chilli, baking powder, chopped parsley and cayenne pepper. Process to a coarse paste, then add the water and season with plenty of salt and pepper. Process again briefly.

3 Heat about 6 cm/2$^{1/2}$ inches of oil in a deep-fat fryer, large, heavy-based saucepan or wok over high heat. Deep-fry rounded tablespoonfuls of the mixture in batches for 2–2$^{1/2}$ minutes until golden and crispy on the outside. Remove with a slotted spoon and drain well on kitchen paper. Serve hot or cold, garnished with parsley sprigs and accompanied by the tahini sauce, pitta bread, yogurt or yogurt dip and lemon wedges.

black bean nachos

ingredients

SERVES 4

225 g/8 oz dried black beans,
    or canned black beans,
    drained

175–225 g/6–8 oz grated
    cheese, such as Cheddar,
    fontina, romano, Asiago,
    or a combination

about 1/4 tsp cumin seeds or
    ground cumin

about 4 tbsp sour cream

thinly sliced pickled jalapeño
    chillies (optional)

1 tbsp chopped fresh
    coriander

handful of shredded lettuce

tortilla chips, to serve

method

1 If using dried black beans, soak the beans overnight, then drain. Put into a pan, cover with water, and bring to the boil. Boil for 10 minutes, then reduce the heat and simmer for 1 1/2 hours, or until tender. Drain well.

2 Spread the beans in a shallow ovenproof dish, then scatter the cheese over the top. Sprinkle with cumin to taste.

3 Bake in a preheated oven, 190°C/375°F/Gas Mark 5, for 10–15 minutes, or until the beans are cooked through and the cheese is bubbly and melted.

4 Remove from the oven and spoon the sour cream on top. Add the chillies, if using, and sprinkle with coriander and lettuce.

5 Arrange the tortilla chips around the beans, placing them in the mixture. Serve the nachos at once.

beans, nuts & tofu

Beans, nuts and tofu are three of the most important ingredients in a vegetarian diet. Beans are full of protein, and come in a variety of shapes and colours, from the dark red kidney bean, named after its distinctive shape, to the white haricot bean. They make a filling, satisfying base for stews and curries. Chickpeas are eaten whole and also ground into flour – try Mixed Vegetable Curry with Chickpea Pancakes. Lentils are a useful substitute for minced meat, so if you love Italian food, try Lentil Bolognese for a new twist on a classic dish.

For maximum nutritional benefit, eat beans and lentils with a grain food such as rice or wholewheat bread – Kidney Bean Risotto is an ideal combination.

Nuts are also packed with goodness, and are beneficial to the nervous system. Serve Nutty Stilton Roast or Vegetable & Hazelnut Loaf with roast potatoes and plenty of vegetables to replace a traditional meat roast.

Tofu has a bland taste that is transformed when it is cooked with strong flavourings, such as garlic and chilli. It comes in blocks that can be cut into smaller chunks and is a low-fat food that is perfect for vegetarians. Buckwheat Noodle Salad with Smoked Tofu is gluten-free, dairy-free and delicious!

mexican three-bean chilli stew

ingredients

SERVES 6

140 g/5 oz each dried black beans, cannellini beans and borlotti beans, soaked overnight in separate bowls in water to cover

2 tbsp olive oil

1 large onion, finely chopped

2 red peppers, deseeded and diced

2 garlic cloves, very finely chopped

$1/2$ tsp cumin seeds, crushed

1 tsp coriander seeds, crushed

1 tsp dried oregano

$1/2$–2 tsp chilli powder

3 tbsp tomato purée

800 g/1 lb 12 oz canned chopped tomatoes

1 tsp sugar

1 tsp salt

625 ml/20 fl oz vegetable stock

3 tbsp chopped fresh coriander

garnish with slices of red onion and small pieces of avocado

method

1 Drain the beans, put in separate saucepans and cover with cold water. Bring to the boil and boil vigorously for 10–15 minutes, then reduce the heat and simmer for 35–45 minutes until just tender. Drain and set aside.

2 Heat the oil in a large, heavy-based saucepan over medium heat. Add the onion and peppers and cook, stirring frequently, for 5 minutes, or until softened.

3 Add the garlic, cumin and coriander seeds and oregano and cook, stirring, for 30 seconds until the garlic is beginning to colour. Add the chilli powder and tomato purée and cook, stirring, for 1 minute. Add the tomatoes, sugar, salt, beans and stock. Bring to the boil, then reduce the heat, cover and simmer, stirring occasionally, for 45 minutes.

4 Stir in the fresh coriander. Ladle into individual warmed bowls and serve at once. Garnish with slices of red onion and small pieces of avocado.

sweet-&-sour vegetables with cashews

ingredients

SERVES 4

1 tbsp vegetable or peanut oil

1 tsp chilli oil

2 onions, sliced

2 carrots, thinly sliced

2 courgettes, thinly sliced

115 g/4 oz broccoli,
    cut into florets

115 g/4 oz white mushrooms,
    sliced

115 g/4 oz small pak choi,
    halved

2 tbsp jaggery or brown sugar

2 tbsp Thai soy sauce

1 tbsp rice vinegar

55 g/2 oz cashews

method

1 Heat both the oils in a preheated wok or frying pan, add the onions, and stir-fry for 1–2 minutes until beginning to soften.

2 Add the carrots, courgettes and broccoli and stir-fry for 2–3 minutes. Add the mushrooms, pak choi, sugar, soy sauce and vinegar and stir-fry for 1–2 minutes.

3 Meanwhile, heat a dry, heavy-based frying pan over high heat, add the cashews and cook, shaking the pan frequently, until lightly toasted. Sprinkle the cashews over the stir-fry and serve immediately.

spicy fragrant black bean chilli

ingredients

SERVES 4

400 g/14 oz dried black
    beans
2 tbsp olive oil
1 onion, chopped
5 garlic cloves, coarsely
    chopped
$1/2$–1 tsp ground cumin
$1/2$–1 tsp mild red chilli powder
1 red pepper, diced
1 carrot, diced
400 g/14 oz fresh tomatoes,
    diced, or canned, chopped
1 bunch fresh coriander,
    coarsely chopped
salt and pepper

method

1 Soak the beans overnight, then drain. Place in a saucepan, cover with water and bring to the boil. Boil for 10 minutes, then reduce the heat and simmer for $1^{1}/_{2}$ hours, or until tender. Drain well, reserving 250 ml/8 fl oz of the cooking liquid.

2 Heat the oil in a frying pan. Add the onion and garlic and cook, stirring occasionally, until the onion is softened.

3 Stir in the cumin and chilli powder and continue to cook for a moment or two. Add the red pepper, carrot and tomatoes. Cook over medium heat for 5 minutes.

4 Add half the coriander and the beans and their reserved liquid. Season with salt and pepper. Simmer for 30–45 minutes, or until well flavoured and thickened.

5 Stir in the remaining coriander, adjust the seasoning, and serve at once.

provençal bean stew

ingredients

SERVES 4

350 g/12 oz dried borlotti
    beans, soaked overnight in
    water to cover

2 tbsp olive oil

2 onions, sliced

2 garlic cloves, finely chopped

1 red pepper, deseeded and
    sliced

1 yellow pepper, deseeded
    and sliced

400 g/14 oz canned chopped
    tomatoes

2 tbsp tomato purée

1 tbsp torn fresh basil leaves

2 tsp chopped fresh thyme

2 tsp chopped fresh rosemary

1 bay leaf

salt and pepper

55 g/2 oz black olives, pitted
    and halved

2 tbsp chopped fresh parsley,
    to garnish

method

1 Drain the beans. Place in a large saucepan, add enough cold water to cover and bring to the boil. Reduce the heat, then cover and simmer for 1¹/₄–1¹/₂ hours until almost tender. Drain, reserving 300 ml/ 10 fl oz of the cooking liquid.

2 Heat the oil in a heavy-based saucepan over medium heat. Add the onions and cook, stirring frequently, for 5 minutes, or until softened. Add the garlic and peppers and cook, stirring occasionally, for 10 minutes.

3 Add the tomatoes and their can juices, the reserved cooking liquid, tomato purée, basil, thyme, rosemary, bay leaf and beans. Season with salt and pepper. Cover and simmer for 40 minutes. Add the olives and simmer for a further 5 minutes. Transfer to a warmed serving dish, sprinkle with the parsley, and serve immediately.

boston beans

ingredients

SERVES 8

500 g/1 lb 2 oz dried
    cannellini beans, soaked
    overnight in water to cover
2 onions, chopped
2 large tomatoes, peeled and
    chopped
2 tsp American mustard
2 tbsp molasses
salt and pepper

method

1 Drain the beans and put in a large saucepan. Add enough cold water to cover and bring to the boil. Reduce the heat and simmer for 15 minutes. Drain, reserving 300 ml/10 fl oz of the cooking liquid. Transfer the beans to a large casserole and add the onions.

2 Return the reserved cooking liquid to the pan and add the tomatoes. Bring to the boil, then reduce the heat and simmer for 10 minutes. Remove from the heat, stir in the mustard and molasses and season with salt and pepper.

3 Pour the mixture into the casserole, stir and bake in a preheated oven, 140°C/275°F/Gas Mark 1, for 5 hours. Serve hot.

baked portobello mushrooms

ingredients

SERVES 4

4 large portobello mushrooms

200 g/7 oz canned red kidney
    beans, drained and rinsed

4 spring onions, chopped

1 fresh red jalapeño chilli,
    deseeded and finely
    chopped

1 tbsp finely grated lemon rind

1 tbsp chopped fresh flatleaf
    parsley, plus extra sprigs
    to garnish

salt and pepper

85 g/3 oz courgette, coarsely
    grated

85 g/3 oz carrots, coarsely
    grated

55 g/2 oz pine nuts, toasted

40 g/1½ oz raisins

300 ml/10 fl oz vegetable
    stock

sauce

150 ml/5 fl oz Greek-style
    yogurt

1 tbsp chopped fresh parsley,
    plus extra to garnish

1 tbsp grated lemon rind

salt and pepper

method

1 Peel the mushrooms and carefully remove the stalks. Trim and rinse the stalks.

2 Put the mushroom stalks, beans, spring onions, chilli, lemon rind, parsley, salt and pepper into a food processor and process for 2 minutes.

3 Scrape the mixture into a bowl and add the courgette, carrots, pine nuts and raisins. Mix well and use to stuff the mushroom cups.

4 Arrange the stuffed mushrooms in an ovenproof dish, pour the stock around them, and cover with foil. Bake in a preheated oven, 180°C/350°F/Gas Mark 4, for 30 minutes, removing the foil for the last 10 minutes of the cooking time.

5 Meanwhile, to make the sauce, blend all the ingredients together in a small serving dish.

6 Serve the mushrooms hot with the sauce, garnished with parsley sprigs.

red & white bean curry

ingredients

SERVES 4

85 g/3 oz red kidney beans

85 g/3 oz haricot beans

55 g/2 oz black-eyed beans

2 tbsp ghee or vegetable oil

1 tsp black mustard seeds

1 tsp cumin seeds

1 onion, finely chopped

1 tsp garlic purée

1 tsp ginger purée

2 tbsp curry paste

2 fresh green chillies,
    deseeded and chopped

400 g/14 oz canned tomatoes

2 tbsp tomato purée

125–150 ml/4–5 fl oz water
    (optional)

salt

2 tbsp chopped fresh
    coriander, plus extra to
    garnish

method

1 Place all the beans in a large bowl, add enough cold water to cover and soak for at least 4 hours or overnight.

2 Drain the beans and place in a large, heavy-based saucepan. Add enough cold water to cover and bring to the boil over high heat. Boil vigorously for 15 minutes, then reduce the heat, cover and simmer for 1 1/2 hours, or until the beans are tender.

3 Heat the ghee in a separate large saucepan. Add the mustard seeds and cumin seeds and cook over low heat, stirring, for 2 minutes, or until they give off their aroma. Add the onion and cook, stirring frequently, for 5 minutes, or until softened. Add the garlic purée, ginger purée, curry paste and chillies and cook, stirring, for 2 minutes. Stir in the tomatoes and their can juices and the tomato purée. If the sauce seems thick, add the water. Break up the tomatoes with a wooden spoon. Season with salt and simmer for 5 minutes.

4 Drain the beans and add them to the sauce, then stir in the chopped coriander. Cover and simmer for a further 30 minutes, or until the beans are tender and the sauce has thickened. Garnish with extra chopped coriander and serve immediately.

kidney bean risotto

ingredients

SERVES 4

4 tbsp olive oil

1 onion, chopped

2 garlic cloves, finely chopped

175 g/6 oz brown rice

625 ml/20 fl oz vegetable
    stock

salt and pepper

1 red pepper, deseeded
    and chopped

2 celery stalks, sliced

225 g/8 oz chestnut
    mushrooms, thinly sliced

425 g/15 oz canned red
    kidney beans, drained
    and rinsed

3 tbsp chopped fresh parsley,
    plus extra to garnish

55 g/2 oz cashews

method

1 Heat half the oil in a large, heavy-based saucepan. Add the onion and cook, stirring occasionally, for 5 minutes, or until softened. Add half the garlic and cook, stirring frequently, for 2 minutes, then add the rice and stir for 1 minute, or until the grains are thoroughly coated with the oil.

2 Add the stock and a pinch of salt and bring to the boil, stirring constantly. Reduce the heat, cover and simmer for 35–40 minutes, or until all the liquid has been absorbed.

3 Meanwhile, heat the remaining oil in a heavy-based frying pan. Add the pepper and celery and cook, stirring frequently, for 5 minutes. Add the sliced mushrooms and the remaining garlic and cook, stirring frequently, for 4–5 minutes.

4 Stir the rice into the frying pan. Add the beans, parsley and cashews. Season with salt and pepper and cook, stirring constantly, until hot. Transfer to a warmed serving dish, sprinkle with extra parsley, and serve at once.

mixed vegetable curry with chickpea pancakes

ingredients

SERVES 4

200 g/7 oz carrots
300 g/10^1/$_2$ oz potatoes
2 tbsp vegetable oil
1^1/$_2$ tsp cumin seeds
seeds from 5 green
  cardamom pods
1^1/$_2$ tsp mustard seeds
2 onions, grated
1 tsp ground turmeric
1 tsp ground coriander
1^1/$_2$ tsp chilli powder
1 bay leaf
1 tbsp grated fresh root
  ginger
2 large garlic cloves, crushed
250 ml/9 fl oz strained
  tomatoes
200 ml/7 fl oz vegetable stock
115 g/4 oz frozen peas
115 g/4 oz frozen spinach
  leaves

chickpea pancakes
225 g/8 oz chickpea flour
1 tsp salt
^{1}/$_2$ tsp baking soda
400 ml/4 fl oz water
vegetable oil, for cooking

method

1 To make the pancakes, sift the flour, salt and baking soda into a large bowl. Make a well in the centre and add the water. Using a balloon whisk, gradually mix the flour into the water to form a smooth batter. Set aside for 15 minutes.

2 Heat enough oil to cover the bottom of a frying pan over medium heat. Add a small quantity of batter to the pan, and cook for 3 minutes on one side, then turn over and cook the other side until golden. Repeat with the remaining batter to make 8 pancakes.

3 Meanwhile, cut the carrots into chunks and the potatoes into quarters. Place in a steamer and steam until just tender.

4 Heat the oil in a large saucepan over medium heat and fry the cumin, cardamom and mustard seeds until they start to sizzle. Add the onions, partially cover, and cook over medium–low heat, stirring frequently, until soft and golden.

5 Add the other spices, bay leaf, ginger and garlic and cook, stirring, for 1 minute. Add the strained tomatoes, stock, carrots and potatoes, partially cover, and cook for 10–15 minutes, or until the vegetables are tender. Add the peas and spinach, then cook for 2–3 minutes. Serve with the warm pancakes.

spinach with chickpeas

ingredients

SERVES 4–6

2 tbsp olive oil

1 large garlic clove, cut in half

1 medium onion,
    chopped finely

$1/2$ tsp cumin

pinch cayenne pepper

pinch turmeric

800 g/1 lb 12 oz canned
    chickpeas, drained
    and rinsed

500 g/18 oz baby spinach
    leaves, rinsed and
    shaken dry

2 pimientos del piquillo,
    drained and sliced

salt and pepper

method

1 Heat the oil in a large, lidded frying pan over medium–high heat. Add the garlic and cook for 2 minutes, or until golden but not brown. Remove with a slotted spoon and discard.

2 Add the onion and cumin, cayenne and turmeric and cook, stirring, for about 5 minutes until soft. Add the chickpeas and stir around until they are lightly coloured with the turmeric and cayenne.

3 Stir in the spinach with just the water clinging to its leaves. Cover and cook for 4–5 minutes until wilted. Uncover, stir in the pimientos del piquillo and continue cooking, stirring gently, until all the liquid evaporates. Season with salt and pepper and serve.

chickpea curry

ingredients

SERVES 4

6 tbsp vegetable oil
2 onions, sliced
1 tsp finely chopped fresh
    root ginger
1 tsp ground cumin
1 tsp ground coriander
1 tsp fresh garlic, crushed
1 tsp chilli powder
2 fresh green chillies
2–3 tbsp fresh coriander
    leaves
150 ml/5 fl oz water
1 large potato
400 g/14 oz canned
    chickpeas, drained
1 tbsp lemon juice

method

1 Heat the vegetable oil in a large, heavy-based saucepan. Add the onions and cook, stirring occasionally, until golden. Reduce the heat, add the ginger, ground cumin, ground coriander, garlic, chilli powder, fresh green chillies and fresh coriander leaves and stir-fry for 2 minutes.

2 Add the water to the mixture in the pan and stir to mix.

3 Using a sharp knife, cut the potato into dice, then add, with the chickpeas, to the pan. Cover and simmer, stirring occasionally, for 5–7 minutes.

4 Sprinkle the lemon juice over the curry. Transfer the chickpea curry to serving dishes and serve hot.

chilli bean cakes with avocado salsa

ingredients

SERVES 4

55 g/2 oz pine nuts

425 g/15 oz canned mixed
    beans, drained and rinsed

1/2 red onion, finely chopped

1 tbsp tomato purée

1/2 fresh red chilli, deseeded
    and finely chopped

55 g/2 oz fresh brown
    breadcrumbs

1 egg, beaten

1 tbsp finely chopped fresh
    coriander

2 tbsp corn oil

1 lime, cut into quarters,
    to garnish

4 toasted wholewheat bread
    rolls, to serve (optional)

salsa

1 avocado, stoned, peeled
    and chopped

100 g/3 1/2 oz tomatoes,
    deseeded and chopped

2 garlic cloves, crushed

2 tbsp finely chopped fresh
    coriander

1 tbsp olive oil

pepper

juice of 1/2 lime

method

1 Heat a non-stick frying pan over medium heat, add the pine nuts and cook, turning, until just browned. Immediately tip into a bowl and set aside.

2 Put the beans into a large bowl and coarsely mash. Add the onion, tomato purée, chilli, pine nuts and half the breadcrumbs and mix well. Add half the egg and the coriander and mash together, adding a little more egg, if needed, to bind the mixture. Form the mixture into 4 flat cakes. Coat with the remaining breadcrumbs, cover and chill in the refrigerator for 30 minutes.

3 To make the salsa, mix all the ingredients together in a serving bowl, cover and chill in the refrigerator until required.

4 Heat the oil in a frying pan over medium heat, add the bean cakes and cook for 4–5 minutes on each side, or until crisp and heated through. Remove from the pan and drain on kitchen paper.

5 Serve each bean cake in a toasted wholewheat roll, if desired, with the salsa, garnished with a lime quarter.

bean burgers

ingredients

SERVES 4

1 tbsp sunflower oil, plus
   extra for brushing

1 onion, finely chopped

1 garlic clove, finely chopped

1 tsp ground coriander

1 tsp ground cumin

115 g/4 oz white mushrooms,
   finely chopped

425 g/15 oz canned borlotti
   or red kidney beans,
   drained and rinsed

2 tbsp chopped fresh flat-leaf
   parsley

salt and pepper

plain flour, for dusting

hamburger buns

salad, to serve

method

1 Heat the oil in a heavy-based frying pan over medium heat. Add the onion and cook, stirring frequently, for 5 minutes, or until softened. Add the garlic, coriander and cumin and cook, stirring, for a further minute. Add the mushrooms and cook, stirring frequently, for 4–5 minutes until all the liquid has evaporated. Transfer to a bowl.

2 Put the beans in a small bowl and mash with a fork. Stir into the mushroom mixture with the parsley and season with salt and pepper.

3 Preheat the grill to medium–high. Divide the mixture equally into 4 portions, dust lightly with flour and shape into flat, round patties. Brush with oil and cook under the grill for 4–5 minutes on each side. Serve in hamburger buns with salad.

toasted pine nut & vegetable couscous

ingredients

SERVES 4

115 g/4 oz dried green lentils
55 g/2 oz pine nuts
1 tbsp olive oil
1 onion, diced
2 garlic cloves, crushed
280 g/10 oz courgettes, sliced
250 g/9 oz tomatoes, chopped
400 g/14 oz canned artichoke
　hearts, drained and cut in
　half lengthways
250 g/9 oz couscous
500 ml/16 fl oz vegetable
　stock
3 tbsp torn fresh basil leaves,
　plus extra leaves to garnish
pepper

method

1 Put the lentils into a saucepan with plenty of cold water, bring to the boil and boil rapidly for 10 minutes. Reduce the heat, cover and simmer for 15 minutes, or until tender.

2 Meanwhile, preheat the grill to medium. Spread the pine nuts out in a single layer on a baking sheet and toast under the preheated grill, turning to brown evenly – watch constantly because they brown very quickly. Tip the pine nuts into a small dish and set aside.

3 Heat the oil in a frying pan over medium heat, add the onion, garlic and courgettes and cook, stirring frequently, for 8–10 minutes, or until tender and the courgettes have browned slightly. Add the tomatoes and artichoke halves and heat through thoroughly for 5 minutes.

4 Meanwhile, put the couscous into a heatproof bowl. Bring the stock to the boil in a saucepan and pour over the couscous, cover and stand for 10 minutes until the couscous absorbs the stock and becomes tender.

5 Drain the lentils and stir into the couscous. Stir in the torn basil leaves and season well with pepper. Transfer to a warmed serving dish and spoon over the cooked vegetables. Sprinkle the pine nuts over the top, garnish with basil leaves and serve at once.

warm red lentil salad with goat's cheese

ingredients

SERVES 4

2 tbsp olive oil

2 tsp cumin seeds

2 garlic cloves, crushed

2 tsp grated fresh root ginger

300 g/10^{1}/$_{2}$ oz split red lentils

750 ml/24 fl oz vegetable
  stock

2 tbsp chopped fresh mint

2 tbsp chopped fresh
  coriander

2 red onions, thinly sliced

200 g/7 oz baby spinach
  leaves

1 tsp hazelnut oil

150 g/5^{1}/$_{2}$ oz soft goat's
  cheese

4 tbsp Greek-style yogurt

pepper

1 lemon, cut into quarters,
  to garnish

toasted rye bread, to serve

method

1 Heat half the olive oil in a large saucepan over medium heat, add the cumin seeds, garlic and ginger and cook for 2 minutes, stirring constantly.

2 Stir in the lentils, then add the stock, a ladleful at a time, until it is all absorbed, stirring constantly – this will take about 20 minutes. Remove from the heat and stir in the herbs.

3 Meanwhile, heat the remaining olive oil in a frying pan over medium heat, add the onions and cook, stirring frequently, for 10 minutes, or until soft and lightly browned.

4 Toss the spinach in the hazelnut oil in a bowl, then divide between 4 serving plates.

5 Mash the goat's cheese with the yogurt in a small bowl and season with pepper.

6 Divide the lentils between the serving plates and top with the onions and goat's cheese mixture. Garnish with lemon quarters and serve with toasted rye bread.

lentil bolognese

ingredients

SERVES 4

1 tsp vegetable oil

1 tsp crushed garlic

25 g/1 oz onion, finely
    chopped

25 g/1 oz leek, finely chopped

25 g/1 oz celery, finely chopped

25 g/1 oz green pepper,
    deseeded and finely
    chopped

25 g/1 oz carrot, finely
    chopped

25 g/1 oz courgette, finely
    chopped

85 g/3 oz flat mushrooms,
    diced

4 tbsp red wine

pinch of dried thyme

400 g/14 oz canned tomatoes,
    chopped, strained through
    a colander, and the juice
    and pulp reserved
    separately

4 tbsp dried Puy or green
    lentils, cooked

pepper, to taste

2 tsp lemon juice

1 tsp sugar

3 tbsp chopped fresh basil,
    plus extra sprigs to garnish

freshly cooked spaghetti,
    to serve

method

1 Heat a saucepan over low heat, add the oil and garlic and cook, stirring, until golden brown. Add all the vegetables, except the mushrooms, increase the heat to medium and cook, stirring occasionally, for 10–12 minutes, or until softened and there is no liquid from the vegetables left in the pan.

2 Add the mushrooms, increase the heat to high, add the wine and cook for 2 minutes. Add the thyme and the juice from the tomatoes and cook until reduced by half.

3 Add the lentils and pepper, stir in the tomatoes and cook for a further 3–4 minutes. Remove the pan from the heat and stir in the lemon juice, sugar and basil.

4 Serve the sauce with freshly cooked spaghetti, garnished with basil sprigs.

lentil, shallot & mushroom pie

ingredients

SERVES 6

175 g/6 oz Puy or green
    lentils

2 bay leaves

6 shallots, sliced

1.25 litres/40 fl oz vegetable
    stock

salt and pepper

4 tbsp butter

225 g/8 oz long-grain rice

8 sheets filo pastry,
    thawed if frozen

2 tbsp chopped fresh parsley

2 tsp chopped fresh fennel
    or savory

4 eggs, 1 beaten and
    3 hard-boiled and sliced

225 g/8 oz portobello
    mushrooms, sliced

method

1 Put the lentils, bay leaves and half the shallots in a large, heavy-based saucepan. Add half the stock and bring to the boil. Reduce the heat and simmer for 25 minutes, or until the lentils are tender. Remove from the heat, season to taste with salt and pepper and cool completely.

2 Melt half the butter in a saucepan over medium heat, add the remaining shallots, and cook, stirring frequently, until softened. Add the rice and cook, stirring, for 1 minute, then add the remaining stock. Season and bring to the boil. Reduce the heat, cover and simmer for 15 minutes. Remove from the heat and cool completely.

3 Melt the remaining butter over low heat, then brush an ovenproof dish with a little of it. Arrange the filo sheets in the dish with the sides overhanging, brushing each sheet with melted butter. Add the parsley, fennel and beaten egg to the rice mixture. Make layers of rice, hard-boiled egg, lentils and mushrooms in the dish, seasoning each layer. Scrunch up the filo sheets into folds on top of the pie. Brush with melted butter and chill for 15 minutes. Bake in a preheated oven, 190°C/ 375°F/Gas Mark 5, for 45 minutes. Let stand for 10 minutes before serving.

baby corn with dal

ingredients

SERVES 4

225 g/8 oz red split lentils

2 tbsp vegetable oil

1 tsp cumin seeds

1 tsp ground coriander

1/2 tsp asafetida

1 fresh red chilli, deseeded
    and finely chopped

115 g/4 oz green beans,
    chopped, blanched
    and drained

1 green pepper, deseeded
    and chopped

115 g/4 oz baby corn, sliced
    diagonally

150 ml/5 fl oz vegetable stock

2 tomatoes, deseeded and
    chopped

1 tbsp chopped fresh
    coriander

1 tbsp poppy seeds

method

1 Rinse the lentils 2–3 times in cold water.
Put into a large saucepan and cover with cold
water. Bring to the boil, then reduce the heat
and simmer for 15–20 minutes, or until tender.
Drain, return to the pan and keep warm.

2 Meanwhile, heat the oil in a separate
saucepan over low heat, add the spices and
chilli and cook for 2 minutes, stirring constantly.
Add the beans, green pepper and baby corn
and cook for 2 minutes, stirring constantly.

3 Stir in the stock and bring to the boil, then
reduce the heat and simmer for 5 minutes, or
until the vegetables are just tender.

4 Stir the vegetables and their liquid into the
cooked lentils with the tomatoes and heat
through for 5–8 minutes, or until piping hot.

5 Serve at once, sprinkled with the coriander
and poppy seeds.

celeriac, chestnut, spinach & feta filo pies

ingredients

SERVES 4

4 tbsp olive oil

2 garlic cloves, crushed

1/2 large or 1 whole small head celeriac, cut into short thin sticks

250 g/9 oz baby spinach leaves

85 g/3 oz cooked, peeled chestnuts, coarsely chopped

200 g/7 oz feta cheese (drained weight), crumbled

1 egg

2 tbsp pesto sauce

1 tbsp finely chopped fresh parsley

pepper

4 sheets filo pastry, about 32 x 18 cm/ 13 x 7 inches each

method

1 Heat 1 tablespoon of the oil in a large frying pan over medium heat, add the garlic and cook for 1 minute, stirring constantly. Add the celeriac and cook for 5 minutes, or until soft and browned. Remove from the pan and keep warm.

2 Add 1 tablespoon of the remaining oil to the frying pan, then add the spinach, cover and cook for 2–3 minutes, or until the spinach has wilted. Uncover and cook until any liquid has evaporated.

3 Mix the garlic and celeriac, spinach, chestnuts, cheese, egg, pesto, parsley and pepper in a large bowl. Divide the mixture between 4 individual gratin dishes or put it all into 1 medium gratin dish.

4 Brush each sheet of filo with the remaining oil and arrange, slightly scrunched, on top of the celeriac mixture. Bake in a preheated oven, 190°C/375°F/Gas Mark 5, for 15–20 minutes, or until browned. Serve at once.

nutty stilton roast

ingredients

SERVES 6–8

2 tbsp virgin olive oil,
    plus extra for oiling

2 onions, one finely chopped
    and one cut into
    thin wedges

3–5 garlic cloves, crushed

2 celery stalks, finely sliced

175 g/6 oz cooked and
    peeled chestnuts

175 g/6 oz mixed chopped
    nuts

55 g/2 oz ground almonds

55 g/2 oz fresh wholewheat
    breadcrumbs

225 g/8 oz Stilton cheese,
    crumbled

1 tbsp chopped fresh basil,
    plus extra sprigs to garnish

1 egg, beaten

salt and pepper

1 red pepper, peeled,
    deseeded and cut into thin
    wedges

1 courgette, about 115 g/
    4 oz, cut into wedges

cherry tomatoes, to garnish

tomato ketchup, to serve

method

1 Heat 1 tablespoon of the oil in a frying pan over medium heat, add the chopped onion, 1–2 of the garlic cloves, and the celery and cook for 5 minutes, stirring occasionally.

2 Remove from the pan, drain through a sieve and transfer to a food processor with the nuts, breadcrumbs, half the cheese and the basil. Using the pulse button, blend the ingredients together, then slowly blend in the egg to form a stiff mixture. Season.

3 Heat the remaining oil in a frying pan over medium heat, add the onion wedges, remaining garlic, red pepper and courgette and cook for 5 minutes, stirring frequently. Remove from the pan, add salt and pepper and drain through a sieve.

4 Place half the nut mixture in a lightly oiled 900-g/2-lb loaf pan and smooth the surface. Cover with the onion and pepper mixture and crumble over the remaining cheese. Top with the remaining nut mixture and press down firmly. Cover with foil. Bake in a preheated oven, 180°C/350°F/Gas Mark 4, for 45 minutes. Remove the foil and bake for a further 25–35 minutes, or until cooked and firm to the touch.

5 Remove from the oven, cool in the pan for 5 minutes, then turn out and serve in slices garnished with basil sprigs, cherry tomatoes and a little tomato ketchup.

vegetable & hazelnut loaf

ingredients

SERVES 4

2 tbsp sunflower oil, plus
    extra for oiling
1 onion, chopped
1 garlic clove, finely chopped
2 celery stalks, chopped
1 tbsp plain flour
200 ml/7 fl oz strained
    canned tomatoes
115 g/4 oz fresh wholewheat
    breadcrumbs
2 carrots, grated
115 g/4 oz toasted hazelnuts,
    ground
1 tbsp dark soy sauce
2 tbsp chopped fresh
    coriander
1 egg, lightly beaten
salt and pepper
mixed red and green lettuce
    leaves, to serve

method

1 Oil and line a 450-g/1-lb loaf pan. Heat the oil in a heavy-based frying pan over medium heat. Add the onion and cook, stirring frequently, for 5 minutes, or until softened. Add the garlic and celery and cook, stirring frequently, for 5 minutes. Add the flour and cook, stirring constantly, for 1 minute. Gradually stir in the strained canned tomatoes and cook, stirring constantly, until thickened. Remove the pan from the heat.

2 Put the breadcrumbs, carrots, ground hazelnuts, soy sauce and coriander in a bowl. Add the tomato mixture and stir well. Cool slightly, then beat in the egg and season with salt and pepper.

3 Spoon the mixture into the prepared pan and smooth the surface. Cover with foil and bake in a preheated oven, 180°C/350°F/Gas Mark 4, for 1 hour. If serving hot, turn the loaf out on to a warmed serving dish and serve immediately with mixed red and green salad leaves. Alternatively, cool the loaf in the pan before turning out.

buckwheat noodle salad with smoked tofu

ingredients

SERVES 2

200 g/7 oz buckwheat noodles

250 g/9 oz firm smoked tofu, drained weight

200 g/7 oz white cabbage, finely shredded

250 g/9 oz carrots, finely shredded

3 spring onions, diagonally sliced

1 fresh red chilli, deseeded and finely sliced into circles

2 tbsp sesame seeds, lightly toasted

dressing

1 tsp grated fresh root ginger

1 garlic clove, crushed

175 g/6 oz silken tofu, drained weight

4 tsp tamari (wheat-free soy sauce)

2 tbsp sesame oil

4 tbsp hot water

salt

method

1 Cook the noodles in a large saucepan of lightly salted boiling water according to the packet instructions. Drain and refresh under cold running water.

2 To make the dressing, blend the ginger, garlic, silken tofu, tamari, oil and water together in a small bowl until smooth and creamy. Season with salt.

3 Place the smoked tofu in a steamer. Steam for 5 minutes, then cut into thin slices.

4 Meanwhile, put the cabbage, carrots, spring onions and chilli into a bowl and toss to mix. To serve, arrange the noodles on serving plates and top with the carrot salad and slices of tofu. Spoon over the dressing and sprinkle with sesame seeds.

thai tofu cakes
with chilli dip

ingredients

SERVES 8

300 g/10^1/$_2$ oz firm tofu,
    drained weight,
    coarsely grated

1 lemon grass stalk, outer layer
    discarded, finely chopped

2 garlic cloves, chopped

2.5-cm/1-inch piece fresh
    root ginger, grated

2 kaffir lime leaves, finely
    chopped (optional)

2 shallots, finely chopped

2 fresh red chillies, deseeded
    and finely chopped

4 tbsp chopped fresh
    coriander

90 g/3^1/$_4$ oz gluten-free plain
    flour, plus extra for flouring

^{1}/$_2$ tsp salt

corn oil, for cooking

chilli dip

3 tbsp white distilled vinegar
    or rice wine vinegar

2 spring onions, finely sliced

1 tbsp caster sugar

2 fresh chillies, finely
    chopped

2 tbsp chopped fresh
    coriander

pinch of salt

method

1 To make the chilli dip, mix all the ingredients together in a small serving bowl and set aside.

2 Mix the tofu with the lemon grass, garlic, ginger, lime leaves, if using, shallots, chillies and coriander in a mixing bowl. Stir in the flour and salt to make a coarse, sticky paste. Cover and chill in the refrigerator for 1 hour to let the mixture firm up slightly.

3 Form the mixture into 8 large walnut-size balls and, using floured hands, flatten into circles. Heat enough oil to cover the bottom of a large, heavy-based frying pan over medium heat. Cook the cakes in 2 batches, turning halfway through, for 4–6 minutes, or until golden brown. Drain on kitchen paper and serve warm with the chilli dip.

spicy tofu

ingredients

SERVES 4

marinade

75 ml/2¹/2 fl oz vegetable
stock
2 tsp cornflour
2 tbsp soy sauce
1 tbsp caster sugar
pinch of chilli flakes

stir-fry

250 g/9 oz firm tofu, rinsed
and drained thoroughly
and cut into
1-cm/¹/2-inch cubes
4 tbsp peanut oil
1 tbsp grated fresh root ginger
3 garlic cloves, crushed
4 spring onions, sliced thinly
1 head of broccoli,
cut into florets
1 carrot, cut into batons
1 yellow pepper,
sliced thinly
250 g/9 oz shiitake
mushrooms, sliced thinly
steamed rice, to serve

method

1 Blend the vegetable stock, cornflour, soy sauce, sugar and chilli flakes together in a large bowl. Add the tofu and toss well to coat. Set aside to marinate for 20 minutes.

2 In a wok, heat 2 tablespoons of the peanut oil and stir-fry the tofu with its marinade until brown and crispy. Remove from the wok and set aside.

3 Heat the remaining 2 tablespoons of peanut oil in the wok and stir-fry the ginger, garlic and spring onions for 30 seconds. Add the broccoli, carrot, yellow pepper and mushrooms to the wok and cook for 5–6 minutes. Return the tofu to the wok and stir-fry to reheat. Serve immediately over steamed rice.

pasta, noodles & rice

Pasta, noodles and rice are always popular and lend themselves perfectly to the vegetarian treatment. The scope for pasta sauces is endless, and here you will find a handful of really special recipes – Fusilli with Gorgonzola & Mushroom Sauce, for example, is rich, stylish and full of flavour, while Pasta with Pesto is a classic, not to be missed. If you've never made your own pesto sauce before, you will be surprised at how easy it is – pick the basil at the last minute for the freshest flavour.

Noodles are wonderful for adding bulk to a stir-fry, but for a different way of serving them, try Sweet-&-Sour Vegetables on Noodle Pancakes, or cook them in stock with vegetables, an excellent recipe for a low-fat diet.

Most cultures throughout the world have a favourite rice dish, and in Italy this is risotto, made with a plump, short-grain rice that releases its starch on cooking to give a creamy result that works wonderfully with vegetables – try the Risotto Primavera, with fresh spring vegetables. Paella is the traditional Spanish rice dish – made with saffron to colour it yellow, it really is the perfect sunshine food. If you like Asian cuisine, try Stir-fried Rice with Green Vegetables from Thailand or Vegetable Biryani, a classic dish from India. You'll never be short of inspiration!

vegetarian lasagna

ingredients

SERVES 4

olive oil, for brushing

2 aubergines, sliced

2 tbsp butter

1 garlic clove, finely chopped

4 courgettes, sliced

1 tbsp finely chopped fresh
    flat-leaf parsley

1 tbsp finely chopped fresh
    marjoram

225 g/8 oz mozzarella
    cheese, grated

625 ml/20 fl oz strained
    canned tomatoes

175 g/6 oz dried no-precook
    lasagna

salt and pepper

béchamel sauce (see below)

55 g/2 oz freshly grated
    Parmesan cheese

béchamel sauce

300 ml/10 fl oz milk

1 bay leaf

6 black peppercorns

slice of onion

mace blade

2 tbsp butter

3 tbsp plain flour

salt and pepper

method

1 To make the béchamel sauce, pour the milk into a saucepan. Add the bay leaf, peppercorns, onion and mace. Heat to just below boiling point, then remove from the heat, cover, infuse for 10 minutes, then strain. Melt the butter in a separate saucepan. Sprinkle in the flour and cook over low heat, stirring constantly, for 1 minute. Gradually stir in the milk, then bring to the boil and cook, stirring, until thickened and smooth. Season with salt and pepper.

2 Brush a grill pan with olive oil and heat until smoking. Add half the aubergine slices and cook over medium heat for 8 minutes, or until golden brown all over. Remove from the grill pan and drain on kitchen paper. Repeat with the remaining aubergine slices.

3 Melt the butter in a frying pan and add the garlic, courgettes, parsley and marjoram. Cook over medium heat, stirring frequently, for 5 minutes, or until the courgettes are golden all over. Remove and drain on kitchen paper.

4 Layer the aubergine, courgettes, mozzarella, tomatoes and lasagna in an ovenproof dish brushed with olive oil, seasoning as you go and finishing with a layer of lasagna. Pour over the béchamel sauce, making sure that all the pasta is covered. Sprinkle with Parmesan cheese and bake in a preheated oven, 200°C/400°F/Gas Mark 6, for 30–40 minutes, or until golden brown. Serve at once.

fusilli with gorgonzola and mushroom sauce

ingredients

SERVES 4

350 g/12 oz dried fusilli

3 tbsp olive oil

350 g/12 oz wild mushrooms
   or white mushrooms, sliced

1 garlic clove, finely chopped

400 ml/14 fl oz double cream

250 g/9 oz Gorgonzola
   cheese, crumbled

salt and pepper

2 tbsp chopped fresh
   flat-leaf parsley, to garnish

method

1 Bring a large saucepan of lightly salted water to the boil. Add the pasta, return to the boil and cook for 8–10 minutes, or until tender but still firm to the bite.

2 Meanwhile, heat the olive oil in a heavy-based pan. Add the mushrooms and cook over low heat, stirring frequently, for 5 minutes. Add the garlic and cook for a further 2 minutes.

3 Add the cream, bring to the boil and cook for 1 minute until slightly thickened. Stir in the cheese and cook over low heat until it has melted. Do not allow the sauce to boil once the cheese has been added. Season with salt and pepper and remove the pan from the heat.

4 Drain the pasta and tip it into the sauce. Toss well to coat, then serve immediately, garnished with the parsley.

chilli broccoli pasta

ingredients

SERVES 4

225 g/8 oz dried penne or
　　macaroni

225 g/8 oz broccoli, cut into
　　florets

50 ml/2 fl oz extra-virgin
　　olive oil

2 large garlic cloves, chopped

2 fresh red chillies, deseeded
　　and diced

8 cherry tomatoes (optional)

fresh basil leaves, to garnish

method

1 Bring a large saucepan of salted boiling
water to the boil. Add the pasta, return to the
boil and cook for 8–10 minutes until tender
but still firm to the bite. Drain the pasta,
refresh under cold running water and drain
again. Set aside.

2 Bring a separate saucepan of salted water
to the boil, add the broccoli and cook for
5 minutes. Drain, refresh under cold running
water and drain again.

3 Heat the oil, in the pan that the pasta was
cooked in, over high heat. Add the garlic,
chillies and tomatoes, if using, and cook,
stirring, for 1 minute.

4 Add the broccoli and mix well. Cook for
2 minutes, stirring, to heat through. Add
the pasta and mix well again. Cook for a
further minute. Transfer the pasta to a large,
warmed serving bowl and serve garnished
with basil leaves.

pasta with pesto

ingredients

SERVES 4

450 g/1 lb dried tagliatelle
fresh basil sprigs, to garnish

pesto

2 garlic cloves
25 g/1 oz pine nuts
salt
115 g/4 oz fresh basil leaves
55 g/2 oz freshly grated
    Parmesan cheese
125 ml/4 fl oz olive oil

method

1 To make the pesto, put the garlic, pine nuts, a large pinch of salt and the basil into a mortar and pound to a paste with a pestle. Transfer to a bowl and gradually work in the Parmesan cheese with a wooden spoon, followed by the olive oil, to make a thick, creamy sauce. Taste and adjust the seasoning if necessary.

2 Alternatively, put the garlic, pine nuts and a large pinch of salt into a food processor or blender and process briefly. Add the basil leaves and process to a paste. With the motor still running, gradually add the olive oil. Scrape into a bowl and beat in the Parmesan cheese.

3 Bring a large pan of lightly salted water to the boil. Add the pasta, return to the boil and cook for 8–10 minutes, or until tender but still firm to the bite. Drain the pasta well, return to the pan, and toss with half the pesto, then divide between warmed serving plates and top with the remaining pesto. Garnish with basil sprigs and serve immediately.

macaroni & cheese

ingredients

SERVES 4

225 g/8 oz macaroni

1 egg, beaten

125 g/4¹/₂ oz mature Cheddar
    cheese, grated

1 tbsp wholegrain mustard

2 tbsp chopped fresh chives

625 ml/20 fl oz béchamel
    sauce (see page 104)

salt and pepper

4 tomatoes, sliced

125 g/4¹/₂ oz Red Leicester
    cheese, grated

60 g/2¹/₄ oz blue cheese, grated

2 tbsp sunflower seeds

snipped fresh chives,
    to garnish

method

1 Bring a large pan of lightly salted water to the boil and cook the macaroni for 8–10 minutes, or until just tender. Drain well and place in an ovenproof dish.

2 Stir the beaten egg, Cheddar cheese, mustard and chives into the béchamel sauce and season with salt and pepper. Spoon the mixture over the macaroni, making sure it is well covered. Top with a layer of the sliced tomatoes.

3 Sprinkle the Red Leicester cheese, blue cheese and sunflower seeds over the top. Place on a baking sheet and bake in a preheated oven, 190°C/375°F/Gas Mark 5, for 25–30 minutes, or until bubbling and golden. Garnish with snipped fresh chives and serve at once.

creamy spinach & mushroom pasta

ingredients

SERVES 4

300 g/10^1/$_2$ oz dried
   gluten-free penne or
   pasta of your choice
2 tbsp olive oil
250 g/9 oz mushrooms, sliced
1 tsp dried oregano
275 ml/9 fl oz vegetable stock
1 tbsp lemon juice
6 tbsp cream cheese
200 g/7 oz frozen spinach
   leaves
salt and pepper

method

1 Cook the pasta in a large pan of lightly salted boiling water, according to the packet instructions. Drain, reserving 175 ml/6 fl oz of the cooking liquid.

2 Meanwhile, heat the oil in a large, heavy-based frying pan over medium heat, add the mushrooms and cook, stirring frequently, for 8 minutes, or until almost crisp. Stir in the oregano, stock and lemon juice and cook for 10–12 minutes, or until the sauce is reduced by half.

3 Stir in the cream cheese and spinach and cook over medium–low heat for 3–5 minutes. Add the reserved cooking liquid, then the cooked pasta. Stir well, season to taste with salt and pepper and heat through gently before serving.

artichoke & olive spaghetti

ingredients

SERVES 4

2 tbsp olive oil

1 large red onion, chopped

2 garlic cloves, crushed

1 tbsp lemon juice

4 baby aubergines, quartered

625 ml/20 fl oz strained
    tomatoes

salt and pepper

2 tsp caster sugar

2 tbsp tomato purée

400 g/14 oz canned artichoke
    hearts, drained and halved

125 g/4$^1/_2$ oz pitted black
    olives

350 g/12 oz wholewheat
    dried spaghetti

fresh basil sprigs, to garnish

olive bread, to serve

method

1 Heat 1 tablespoon of the oil in a large frying pan and gently cook the onion, garlic, lemon juice and aubergines for 4–5 minutes, or until lightly browned.

2 Pour in the strained tomatoes, season with salt and pepper and add the sugar and tomato purée. Bring to the boil, reduce the heat and simmer for 20 minutes. Gently stir in the artichoke halves and olives, and cook for 5 minutes.

3 Meanwhile, bring a large, heavy-based pan of lightly salted water to the boil. Add the spaghetti, return to the boil and cook for 8–10 minutes, or until just tender, but still firm to the bite. Drain well, toss in the remaining olive oil and season with salt and pepper.

4 Transfer the spaghetti to a warmed serving bowl and top with the vegetable sauce. Garnish with the basil sprigs and serve with olive bread.

radiatore with pumpkin sauce

ingredients

SERVES 4

4 tbsp unsalted butter

115 g/4 oz white onions or
    shallots, very finely chopped

salt and pepper

800 g/1 lb 12 oz pumpkin,
    unprepared weight

pinch of freshly grated nutmeg

350 g/12 oz dried radiatore

200 ml/7 fl oz cup single
    cream

4 tbsp freshly grated
    Parmesan cheese,
    plus extra to serve

2 tbsp chopped fresh
    flat-leaf parsley, plus extra
    to garnish

method

1 Melt the butter in a heavy-based pan over low heat. Add the onions, sprinkle with a little salt, cover and cook, stirring frequently, for 25–30 minutes.

2 Scoop out and discard the seeds from the pumpkin. Peel and finely chop the flesh. Tip the pumpkin into the pan and season with nutmeg. Cover and cook over low heat, stirring occasionally, for 45 minutes.

3 Meanwhile, bring a large pan of lightly salted water to the boil. Add the pasta, return to the boil and cook for 8–10 minutes, or until tender but still firm to the bite. Drain thoroughly, reserving about 150 ml/5 fl oz of the cooking liquid.

4 Stir the cream, grated Parmesan cheese and parsley into the pumpkin sauce and season with salt and pepper. If the mixture seems a little too thick, add some or all of the reserved cooking liquid and stir. Tip in the pasta and toss for 1 minute. Serve at once, garnished with chopped parsley, with extra Parmesan cheese for sprinkling.

crisp noodle & vegetable stir-fry

ingredients

SERVES 4

peanut or sunflower oil,
    for deep-frying

115 g/4 oz rice vermicelli,
    broken into 7.5-cm/
    3-inch lengths

115 g/4 oz green beans,
    cut into short lengths

2 carrots, cut into thin sticks

2 courgettes, cut into thin
    sticks

115 g/4 oz shiitake
    mushrooms, sliced

2.5-cm/1-inch piece fresh
    root ginger, shredded

1/2 small head Napa cabbage,
    shredded

4 spring onions, shredded

85 g/3 oz beansprouts

2 tbsp dark soy sauce

2 tbsp Chinese rice wine

large pinch of sugar

2 tbsp coarsely chopped
    fresh coriander

method

1 Half-fill a wok or deep, heavy-based frying pan with oil. Heat to 180–190°C/350–375°F, or until a cube of bread browns in 30 seconds.

2 Add the noodles, in batches, and cook for 1 1/2–2 minutes, or until crisp and puffed up. Remove and drain on kitchen paper. Pour off all but 2 tablespoons of oil from the wok.

3 Heat the remaining oil over high heat. Add the green beans and stir-fry for 2 minutes. Add the carrot and courgette sticks, sliced mushrooms and ginger and stir-fry for a further 2 minutes.

4 Add the shredded Napa cabbage, spring onions and beansprouts and stir-fry for a further minute. Add the soy sauce, rice wine and sugar and cook, stirring constantly, for 1 minute.

5 Add the chopped coriander and toss well. Serve immediately, with the noodles.

chinese vegetables & bean sprouts with noodles

ingredients

SERVES 4

1.25 litres/40 fl oz vegetable
    stock
1 garlic clove, crushed
1-cm/$1/2$-inch piece fresh root
    ginger, finely chopped
225 g/8 oz dried medium
    egg noodles
1 red pepper, deseeded
    and sliced
85 g/3 oz frozen peas
115 g/4 oz broccoli florets
85 g/3 oz shiitake
    mushrooms, sliced
2 tbsp sesame seeds
225 g/8 oz canned water
    chestnuts, drained
    and halved
225 g/8 oz canned bamboo
    shoots, drained
280 g/10 oz Napa cabbage,
    sliced
140 g/5 oz beansprouts
3 spring onions, sliced
1 tbsp dark soy sauce
pepper

method

1 Bring the stock, garlic and ginger to the boil in a large saucepan. Stir in the noodles, red pepper, peas, broccoli and mushrooms and return to the boil. Reduce the heat, cover, and simmer for 5–6 minutes, or until the noodles are tender.

2 Meanwhile, preheat the grill to medium. Spread the sesame seeds out in a single layer on a baking sheet and toast under the preheated grill, turning to brown evenly – watch constantly because they brown very quickly. Tip the sesame seeds into a small dish and set aside.

3 Once the noodles are tender, add the water chestnuts, bamboo shoots, Napa cabbage, beansprouts and spring onions to the pan. Return the stock to the boil, stir to mix the ingredients and simmer for a further 2–3 minutes to heat through thoroughly.

4 Carefully drain off 300 ml/10 fl oz of the stock into a small heatproof jug and set aside. Drain and discard any remaining stock and turn the noodles and vegetables into a warmed serving dish. Quickly mix the soy sauce with the reserved stock and pour over the noodles and vegetables. Season with pepper and serve at once.

sweet-&-sour vegetables on noodle pancakes

ingredients

SERVES 4

115 g/4 oz dried thin
cellophane noodles

6 eggs

4 spring onions, sliced
diagonally

salt and pepper

2$\frac{1}{2}$ tbsp peanut or corn oil

900 g/2 lb selection of
vegetables, such as carrots,
baby corn, cauliflower,
broccoli, mangetout
and onions, peeled as
necessary and chopped
into same-size pieces

100 g/3$\frac{1}{2}$ oz canned bamboo
shoots, drained

200 g/7 oz bottled sweet-&-
sour sauce

method

1 Soak the noodles in enough lukewarm water to cover and stand for 20 minutes, until soft. Alternatively, cook according to the packet instructions. Drain them well and use scissors to cut into 7.5-cm/3-inch pieces, then set aside.

2 Beat the eggs, then stir in the noodles, spring onions, salt and pepper. Heat a 20-cm/8-inch frying pan over high heat. Add 1 tablespoon oil and swirl it round. Pour in a quarter of the egg mixture and tilt the pan so it covers the bottom. Lower the heat to medium and cook for 1 minute, or until the thin pancake is set. Flip it over, adding a little extra oil, if necessary, and cook the other side until golden. Keep warm in a low oven while you make 3 more pancakes.

3 After you've made 4 pancakes, heat a wok or large, heavy-based frying pan over high heat. Add 1$\frac{1}{2}$ tablespoons oil and heat until it shimmers. Add the thickest vegetables, such as carrots, first and stir-fry for 30 seconds. Gradually add the remaining vegetables and bamboo shoots. Stir in the sauce and stir-fry until all the vegetables are tender and the sauce is hot. Spoon the vegetables and sauce over the pancakes and serve.

crunchy walnut risotto

ingredients

SERVES 4

1 tbsp olive oil

70 g/2½ oz butter

1 small onion,
    finely chopped

280 g/10 oz Arborio rice

1.25 litres/40 fl oz simmering
    vegetable stock

salt and pepper

115 g/4 oz walnut halves

85 g/3 oz freshly grated
    Parmesan or Grana
    Padano cheese

55 g/2 oz Mascarpone cheese

55 g/2 oz Gorgonzola cheese,
    diced

method

1 Heat the oil with 2 tablespoons of the butter in a deep pan over medium heat until the butter has melted. Add the onion and cook, stirring occasionally, for 5–7 minutes, or until soft and starting to turn golden. Do not brown.

2 Reduce the heat, add the rice and mix to coat in oil and butter. Cook, stirring constantly, for 2–3 minutes, or until the grains are translucent.

3 Gradually add the hot stock, a ladleful at a time. Stir constantly and add more liquid as the rice absorbs each addition. Increase the heat to medium so that the liquid bubbles. Cook for 20 minutes, or until all the liquid is absorbed and the rice is creamy. Season with salt and pepper.

4 Melt 2 tablespoons of the remaining butter in a frying pan over medium heat. Add the walnuts and toss for 2–3 minutes, or until just starting to brown.

5 Remove the risotto from the heat and add the remaining butter. Mix well, then stir in the Parmesan, Mascarpone and Gorgonzola until they melt, along with most of the walnuts. Spoon the risotto onto warmed plates, sprinkle with the remaining walnuts and serve.

wild mushroom risotto

ingredients

SERVES 6

55 g/2 oz dried porcini or
    morel mushrooms
about 500 g/1 lb 2 oz mixed
    fresh wild mushrooms,
    such as porcini, horse
    mushrooms and
    chanterelles, halved
    if large
4 tbsp olive oil
3–4 garlic cloves,
    finely chopped
55 g/2 oz butter
1 onion, finely chopped
350 g/12 oz Arborio rice
50 ml/2 fl oz dry
    white vermouth
1.25 litres/40 fl oz simmering
    vegetable stock
salt and pepper
115 g/4 oz freshly grated
    Parmesan cheese
4 tbsp chopped fresh
    flat-leaf parsley

method

1 Place the dried mushrooms in a heatproof bowl and add boiling water to cover. Set aside to soak for 30 minutes, then carefully lift out and pat dry. Strain the soaking liquid through a sieve lined with kitchen paper and set aside.

2 Trim the fresh mushrooms and gently brush clean. Heat 3 tablespoons of the oil in a large frying pan. Add the fresh mushrooms and stir-fry for 1–2 minutes. Add the garlic and the soaked mushrooms and cook, stirring frequently, for 2 minutes. Transfer to a plate.

3 Heat the remaining oil and half the butter in a pan. Add the onion and cook over medium heat, stirring, until softened. Reduce the heat, add the rice and cook, stirring, until the grains are translucent. Add the vermouth and cook, stirring, for 1 minute until reduced.

4 Gradually add the hot stock, a ladleful at a time. Stir constantly and add more liquid as the rice absorbs each addition. Increase the heat to medium so that the liquid bubbles. Cook for 20 minutes, or until all the liquid is absorbed and the rice is creamy.

5 Add half the reserved mushroom soaking liquid and stir in the mushrooms. Season and add more mushroom liquid, if necessary. Remove from the heat, stir in the remaining butter, the grated Parmesan and the chopped parsley and serve at once.

risotto primavera

ingredients

SERVES 6–8

225 g/8 oz fresh thin
asparagus spears

4 tbsp olive oil

175 g/6 oz young green
beans, cut into 2.5-cm/
1-inch lengths

175 g/6 oz young courgettes,
quartered and cut into
2.5-cm/1-inch lengths

225 g/8 oz shelled
fresh peas

1 onion, finely chopped

1–2 garlic cloves, finely
chopped

350 g/12 oz Arborio rice

1.6 litres/52 fl oz simmering
vegetable stock

4 spring onions, cut into
2.5-cm/1-inch lengths

salt and pepper

55 g/2 oz butter

115 g/4 oz freshly grated
Parmesan cheese

2 tbsp snipped fresh chives

2 tbsp shredded fresh basil

spring onions, to garnish
(optional)

method

1 Trim the woody ends of the asparagus and cut off the tips. Cut the stems into 2.5-cm/1-inch pieces and set aside with the tips.

2 Heat 2 tablespoons of the oil in a large frying pan over high heat until very hot. Add the asparagus, beans, courgettes and peas and stir-fry for 3–4 minutes until they are bright green and just starting to soften. Set aside.

3 Heat the remaining oil in a large, heavy-based pan over medium heat. Add the onion and cook, stirring occasionally, for 3 minutes, or until it starts to soften. Stir in the garlic and cook, while stirring, for 30 seconds. Reduce the heat, add the rice and mix to coat in oil. Cook, stirring constantly, for 2–3 minutes, or until the grains are translucent.

4 Gradually add the hot stock, a ladleful at a time. Stir constantly and add more liquid as the rice absorbs each addition. Increase the heat to medium so that the liquid bubbles. Cook for 20 minutes, or until all but 2 tablespoons of the liquid is absorbed and the rice is creamy.

5 Stir in the stir-fried vegetables, onion mixture and spring onions with the remaining stock. Cook for 2 minutes, stirring frequently, then season with salt and pepper. Stir in the butter, Parmesan, chives and basil. Remove the pan from the heat and serve the risotto at once, garnished with spring onions, if liked.

spiced risotto cakes

ingredients

SERVES 3

85 g/3 oz onion, finely
    chopped
85 g/3 oz leek, finely chopped
25 g/1 oz Arborio rice
550 ml/18 fl oz vegetable stock
85 g/3 oz grated courgette
1 tbsp fresh basil, chopped
25 g/1 oz fresh wholewheat
    breadcrumbs
vegetable oil spray
radicchio leaves, to serve

filling
50 g/1¾ oz cream cheese
50 g/1¾ oz mango, diced
1 tsp finely grated lime rind
1 tsp lime juice
pinch of cayenne pepper

method

1 Heat a large, non-stick pan over high heat,
add the onion and leek, and cook, stirring
constantly, for 2–3 minutes, or until softened but
not coloured.

2 Add the rice and stock, bring to the boil,
then continue to boil, stirring constantly, for
2 minutes. Reduce the heat and cook for a
further 15 minutes, stirring every 2–3 minutes.
When the rice is nearly cooked and has absorbed
all the stock, stir in the courgette and basil and
cook, continuing to stir, over high heat for a
further 5–10 minutes or until the mixture is
sticky and dry. Turn out onto a plate and let cool.

3 Meanwhile, to make the filling, mix the
cream cheese, mango, lime rind and juice and
cayenne together in a bowl.

4 Divide the cooled rice mixture into 3 and
form into cakes. Make an indentation in the
centre of each cake and fill with 1 tablespoon
of the filling. Mould the sides up and over to
seal in the filling, then reshape with a palette
knife. Coat each cake with breadcrumbs and
arrange on a non-stick baking sheet. Spray
each cake lightly with oil and bake in a
preheated oven, 200°C/400°F/Gas Mark 6, for
15–20 minutes, or until a light golden brown
colour. Serve with radicchio leaves.

stir-fried rice with green vegetables

ingredients

SERVES 4

225 g/8 oz jasmine rice

2 tbsp vegetable or peanut oil

1 tbsp green curry paste

6 spring onions, sliced

2 garlic cloves, crushed

1 courgette, cut into thin
    sticks

115 g/4 oz green beans

175 g/6 oz asparagus,
    trimmed

3–4 fresh Thai basil leaves

method

1 Cook the rice in lightly salted boiling water for 12–15 minutes, drain well, then cool thoroughly and chill overnight.

2 Heat the oil in a wok and stir-fry the curry paste for 1 minute. Add the spring onions and garlic and stir-fry for 1 minute.

3 Add the courgette, beans and asparagus and stir-fry for 3–4 minutes, until just tender. Break up the rice and add it to the wok. Cook, stirring constantly for 2–3 minutes, until the rice is hot. Stir in the basil leaves. Serve hot.

brown rice vegetable pilaf

ingredients

SERVES 4

4 tbsp vegetable oil

1 red onion, finely chopped

2 tender celery stalks, leaves
    included, quartered
    lengthways and diced

2 carrots, coarsely grated

1 fresh green chilli, deseeded
    and finely chopped

3 spring onions, green part
    included, finely chopped

40 g/1^1/$_2$ oz whole almonds,
    sliced lengthways

350 g/12 oz cooked brown
    basmati rice

150 g/5^1/$_2$ oz split red lentils,
    cooked

175 ml/6 fl oz vegetable stock

5 tbsp fresh orange juice

salt and pepper

fresh celery leaves, to garnish

method

1 Heat 2 tablespoons of the oil, in a high-sided
frying pan with a lid, over medium heat. Add
the onion. Cook for 5 minutes, or until softened.

2 Add the celery, carrots, chilli, spring onions
and almonds. Stir-fry for 2 minutes, or until
the vegetables are al dente but still brightly
coloured. Transfer to a bowl and set aside
until required.

3 Add the remaining oil to the pan. Stir in the
rice and lentils. Cook over medium-high heat,
stirring, for 1–2 minutes, or until heated through.
Reduce the heat. Stir in the stock and orange
juice. Season with salt and pepper.

4 Return the vegetables to the pan. Toss with
the rice for a few minutes until heated through.
Transfer to a warmed dish, garnish with celery
leaves and serve.

artichoke paella

ingredients

SERVES 4–6

1/2 tsp saffron threads

2 tbsp hot water

3 tbsp olive oil

1 large onion, chopped

1 courgette, coarsely
    chopped

2 garlic cloves, crushed

1/4 tsp cayenne pepper

225 g/8 oz tomatoes, peeled
    and cut into wedges

425 g/15 oz canned
    chickpeas, drained

425 g/15 oz canned
    artichokes hearts, drained
    and coarsely sliced

350 g/12 oz medium-grain
    paella rice

1.3 litres/42 fl oz simmering
    vegetable stock

150 g/5 1/2 oz green beans,
    blanched

salt and pepper

1 lemon, cut into wedges,
    to serve

method

1 Put the saffron threads and water in a small bowl and infuse for a few minutes.

2 Meanwhile, heat the oil in a paella pan and cook the onion and courgette over medium heat, stirring, for 2–3 minutes, or until softened. Add the garlic, cayenne pepper and saffron and its soaking liquid and cook, stirring constantly, for 1 minute. Add the tomato wedges, chickpeas and artichokes and cook, stirring, for a further 2 minutes.

3 Add the rice and cook, stirring constantly, for 1 minute, or until the rice is glossy and coated. Pour in most of the hot stock and bring to the boil, then simmer, uncovered, for 10 minutes. Do not stir during cooking, but shake the pan once or twice. Add the green beans and season. Shake the pan and cook for a further 10–15 minutes, or until the rice grains are plump and cooked. If the liquid is absorbed too quickly, pour in a little more hot stock, then shake the pan to spread the liquid through the paella.

4 When all the liquid has been absorbed and you detect a faint toasty aroma coming from the rice, remove from the heat immediately to prevent burning. Cover the pan with a clean tea towel or foil and let stand for 5 minutes. Serve direct from the pan with the lemon wedges to squeeze over the rice.

vegetarian paella

ingredients

SERVES 4–6

1/2 tsp saffron threads

2 tbsp hot water

6 tbsp olive oil

1 Spanish onion, sliced

3 garlic cloves, minced

1 red pepper, deseeded and
    sliced

1 orange pepper, deseeded
    and sliced

1 large aubergine, cubed

200 g/7 oz medium-grain
    paella rice

625 ml/20 fl oz vegetable
    stock

450 g/1 lb tomatoes, peeled
    and chopped

salt and pepper

115 g/4 oz mushrooms, sliced

115 g/4 oz green beans, halved

400 g/14 oz canned
    borlotti beans

method

1 Put the saffron threads and water in a small bowl or cup and infuse for a few minutes.

2 Meanwhile, heat the oil in a paella pan or wide, shallow frying pan and cook the onion over medium heat, stirring, for 2–3 minutes, or until softened. Add the garlic, peppers and aubergine and cook, stirring frequently, for 5 minutes.

3 Add the rice and cook, stirring constantly, for 1 minute, or until glossy and coated. Pour in the stock and add the tomatoes, saffron and its soaking water, salt and pepper. Bring to the boil, then reduce the heat and simmer, shaking the pan frequently and stirring occasionally, for 15 minutes.

4 Stir in the mushrooms, green beans and borlotti beans with their can juices. Cook for a further 10 minutes, then serve immediately.

paella de verduras

ingredients

SERVES 4–6

1/2 tsp saffron threads

2 tbsp hot water

3 tbsp olive oil

1 large onion, chopped

2 garlic cloves, crushed

1 tsp paprika

225 g/8 oz tomatoes, peeled
and cut into wedges

1 red pepper, halved and
deseeded, then grilled,
peeled and sliced

1 green pepper, halved and
deseeded, then grilled,
peeled and sliced

425 g/15 oz canned
chickpeas, drained

350 g/12 oz medium-grain
paella rice

1.3 litres/42 fl oz simmering
vegetable stock

55 g/2 oz shelled peas

150 g/5 1/2 oz fresh asparagus
spears, blanched

salt and pepper

1 tbsp chopped fresh flat-leaf
parsley, plus extra
to garnish

1 lemon, cut into wedges,
to serve (optional)

method

1 Put the saffron threads and water in a small bowl and infuse for a few minutes.

2 Meanwhile, heat the oil in a paella pan and cook the onion over medium heat, stirring, for 2–3 minutes, or until softened. Add the garlic, paprika and saffron and its soaking liquid and cook, stirring, for 1 minute. Add the tomatoes, peppers and chickpeas and cook, stirring, for a further 2 minutes.

3 Add the rice and cook, stirring constantly, for 1 minute or until glossy and coated. Pour in most of the hot stock and bring to the boil. Reduce the heat and simmer, uncovered, for 10 minutes. Do not stir during cooking, but shake the pan once or twice. Add the peas, asparagus and parsley and season with salt and pepper. Shake the pan and cook for a further 10–15 minutes, or until the rice grains are plump and cooked. Pour in a little more hot stock if necessary, then shake the pan to spread the liquid through the paella.

4 When all the liquid has been absorbed and you detect a faint toasty aroma coming from the rice, remove from the heat immediately to prevent burning. Cover the pan with a clean tea towel or foil and let stand for 5 minutes. Sprinkle over chopped parsley to garnish and serve direct from the pan with the lemon wedges for squeezing over the rice, if using.

vegetable biryani

ingredients

SERVES 4

2 tbsp vegetable oil

3 whole cloves

3 cardamom pods, cracked

1 onion, chopped

115 g/4 oz carrots, chopped

2–3 garlic cloves, crushed

1–2 fresh red chillies,
    deseeded and chopped

2.5-cm/1-inch piece fresh
    root ginger, grated

115 g/4 oz cauliflower, broken
    into small florets

175 g/6 oz broccoli, broken
    into small florets

115 g/4 oz green beans,
    chopped

400 g/14 oz canned chopped
    tomatoes

150 ml/5 fl oz vegetable stock

salt and pepper

115 g/4 oz okra, sliced

1 tbsp chopped fresh
    coriander, plus extra
    sprigs to garnish

115 g/4 oz brown basmati
    rice

few saffron threads (optional)

grated lime rind, to garnish

method

1 Heat the oil in a large pan over low heat, add the spices, onion, carrots, garlic, chillies and ginger and cook, stirring frequently, for 5 minutes.

2 Add the cauliflower, broccoli and green beans and cook, stirring frequently, for 5 minutes. Stir in the tomatoes, stock, salt and pepper and bring to the boil. Reduce the heat, cover and simmer for 10 minutes.

3 Add the okra and cook for a further 8–10 minutes, or until the vegetables are tender. Stir in the coriander. Strain off any excess liquid and keep warm.

4 Meanwhile, cook the rice with the saffron in a pan of lightly salted boiling water for 25 minutes, or until tender. Drain and keep warm.

5 Layer the vegetables and cooked rice in a deep dish or ovenproof bowl, packing the layers down firmly. Let stand for about 5 minutes, then invert onto a warmed serving dish and serve, garnished with grated lime rind and coriander sprigs, with the reserved liquid.

stuffed red peppers with basil

ingredients

SERVES 4

140 g/5 oz long-grain
   white or brown rice
4 large red peppers
2 tbsp olive oil
1 garlic clove, chopped
4 shallots, chopped
1 celery stalk, chopped
3 tbsp chopped
   toasted walnuts
2 tomatoes, peeled
   and chopped
1 tbsp lemon juice
50 g/1^3/4 oz raisins
4 tbsp freshly grated
   Cheddar cheese
2 tbsp chopped fresh basil
salt and pepper
fresh basil sprigs, to garnish
lemon wedges, to serve

method

1 Cook the rice in a pan of lightly salted boiling water for 20 minutes, if using white rice, or 35 minutes, if using brown. Drain, rinse under cold running water, then drain again.

2 Using a sharp knife, cut the tops off the peppers and set aside. Remove the seeds and white cores, then blanch the peppers and reserved tops in boiling water for 2 minutes. Remove from the heat and drain well. Heat half the oil in a large frying pan. Add the garlic and shallots and cook, stirring, for 3 minutes. Add the celery, walnuts, tomatoes, lemon juice and raisins and cook for a further 5 minutes. Remove from the heat and stir in the cheese, chopped basil, salt and pepper.

3 Stuff the peppers with the rice mixture and arrange them in a baking dish. Place the tops on the peppers, drizzle over the remaining oil, loosely cover with foil, and bake in a preheated oven, 180°C/350°F/Gas Mark 4, for 45 minutes. Remove from the oven, garnish with basil sprigs and serve with lemon wedges.

vegetables
& salads

Vegetables are an essential part of any diet and there are endless ways of using them to add variety and interest. Potatoes are very homely and comforting, and marry well with cheese – Potato & Cheese Gratin and Potato-topped Vegetables, served golden and bubbling from the oven, are both absolutely gorgeous, while Stuffed Baked Potatoes make a simple, inexpensive midweek family dish.

There are some great ideas in this section for entertaining. Mushroom Stroganoff is rich and creamy – use a good selection of mushrooms for the best effect. Cherry Tomato Clafoutis, Potato, Fontina & Rosemary Tart and Roasted Squash Wedges, served with an unusual three-grain risotto mix, are bound to impress, too.

To encourage anyone who thinks they don't like vegetables, try serving some extra special side dishes. Roasted Garlic Creamed Potatoes turn what can be a rather bland offering into a taste sensation; Stir-fried Broccoli is quite fabulous with a light coating of root ginger and chilli sauce; and Brussels Sprouts with Chestnuts and Roasted Onions are perfect to accompany a nut roast.

Salad vegetables are a great source of vitamins, and avocados are a highly nutritious superfood for vegetarians. Put the two together in an Avocado Salad with Lime Dressing – just heaven!

potato & cheese gratin

ingredients

SERVES 4–6

900 g/2 lb waxy potatoes,
    peeled and thinly sliced
1 large garlic clove, halved
butter, for greasing and
    dotting over the top
225 ml/8 fl oz double cream
freshly grated nutmeg
salt and pepper
175 g/6 oz Gruyère cheese,
    finely grated

method

1 Put the potato slices in a bowl, cover with cold water and let stand for 5 minutes, then drain well.

2 Meanwhile, rub the bottom and sides of an oval gratin or ovenproof dish with the cut sides of the garlic halves, pressing down firmly to impart the flavour. Lightly grease the sides of the dish with butter.

3 Place the potatoes in a bowl with the cream and season with freshly grated nutmeg, salt and pepper. Use your hands to mix everything together, then transfer the potatoes to the gratin dish and pour over any cream remaining in the bowl.

4 Sprinkle the cheese over the top and dot with butter. Place the gratin dish on a baking sheet and bake in a preheated oven, 190°C/375°F/Gas Mark 5, for 60–80 minutes, or until the potatoes are tender when pierced with a skewer and the top is golden and bubbling. Let stand for about 2 minutes, then serve straight from the gratin dish.

potato, fontina & rosemary tart

ingredients

SERVES 4

1 quantity puff pastry

plain flour, for dusting

filling

3–4 waxy potatoes

300 g/10^1/$_2$ oz fontina
    cheese, cut into cubes

1 red onion, thinly sliced

3 large fresh rosemary sprigs

2 tbsp olive oil

salt and pepper

1 egg yolk

method

1 Roll out the dough on a lightly floured counter into a circle about 25 cm/10 inches in diameter and put on a baking sheet.

2 Slice the potatoes as thinly as possible so that they are almost transparent – use a mandolin if you have one. Arrange the potato slices in a spiral, overlapping the slices to cover the pastry, leaving a 2-cm/3/4-inch margin around the edge.

3 Arrange the cheese and onion over the potatoes, sprinkle with the rosemary and drizzle over the oil. Season to taste with salt and pepper and brush the edges with the egg yolk to glaze.

4 Bake in a preheated oven, 190°C/375°F/Gas Mark 5, for 25 minutes, or until the potatoes are tender and the pastry is brown and crisp. Serve hot.

potato-topped vegetables

ingredients

SERVES 4

1 carrot, diced

175 g/6 oz cauliflower florets

175 g/6 oz broccoli florets

1 fennel bulb, sliced

75 g/2³/4 oz green beans,
    halved

2 tbsp butter

2¹/2 tbsp plain flour

150 ml/5 fl oz vegetable stock

150 ml/5 fl oz dry white wine

150 ml/5 fl oz milk

175 g/6 oz chestnut
    mushrooms, cut into
    quarters

2 tbsp chopped fresh sage

salt and pepper

topping

900 g/2 lb diced floury
    potatoes

2 tbsp butter

4 tbsp plain yogurt

75 g/2¹/2 oz freshly grated
    Parmesan cheese

1 tsp fennel seeds

method

1 Cook the carrot, cauliflower, broccoli, fennel and beans in a large saucepan of boiling water for 10 minutes, until just tender. Drain the vegetables thoroughly and set aside.

2 Melt the butter in a saucepan. Stir in the flour and cook for 1 minute. Remove from the heat and stir in the stock, wine and milk. Return to the heat and bring to the boil, stirring until thickened. Stir in the reserved vegetables, mushrooms and sage and season with salt and pepper.

3 Meanwhile, make the topping. Cook the diced potatoes in a saucepan of boiling water for 10–15 minutes. Drain and mash with the butter, yogurt and half the Parmesan cheese. Stir in the fennel seeds.

4 Spoon the vegetable mixture into a 1-litre/32-fl oz pie dish. Spoon the potato over the top and sprinkle with the remaining cheese. Cook in a preheated oven, 190°C/375°F/Gas Mark 5, for 30–35 minutes, until golden.

stuffed baked potatoes

ingredients

SERVES 4

900 g/2 lb baking potatoes,
    scrubbed

2 tbsp vegetable oil

1 tsp coarse sea salt

115 g/4 oz butter

1 small onion, chopped

salt and pepper

115 g/4 oz grated Cheddar
    cheese or crumbled
    Stilton cheese

snipped fresh chives,
    to garnish

optional

4 tbsp canned, drained
    corn kernels

4 tbsp cooked mushrooms,
    courgettes or peppers

method

1 Prick the potatoes in several places with a fork and put on a baking sheet. Brush with the oil and sprinkle with the salt. Bake in a preheated oven, 190°C/375°F/Gas Mark 5, for 1 hour, or until the skins are crispy and the insides are soft when pierced with a fork.

2 Meanwhile, melt 1 tablespoon of the butter in a small frying pan over medium–low heat. Add the onion and cook, stirring occasionally, for 8–10 minutes until soft and golden. Set aside.

3 Cut the potatoes in half lengthways. Scoop the flesh into a large bowl, leaving the skins intact. Set aside the skins. Increase the oven temperature to 200°C/400°F/Gas Mark 6.

4 Coarsely mash the potato flesh and mix in the onion and remaining butter. Add salt and pepper to taste and stir in any of the optional ingredients. Spoon the mixture back into the reserved potato skins. Top with the cheese.

5 Cook the filled potato skins in the oven for 10 minutes, or until the cheese has melted and is beginning to brown. Garnish with chives and serve immediately.

roasted ratatouille & potato wedges

ingredients

SERVES 4

300 g/10^1/$_2$ oz potatoes in
    their skins, scrubbed
200 g/7 oz aubergine, cut into
    ^{1}/$_2$-inch/1-cm wedges
125 g/4^1/$_2$ oz red onion cut
    into 5-mm/^{1}/$_4$-inch slices
200 g/7 oz deseeded mixed
    peppers, sliced into
    1-cm/^{1}/$_2$-inch strips
175 g/6 oz courgettes, cut in
    half lengthwise, then into
    1-cm/^{1}/$_2$-inch slices
125 g/4^1/$_2$ oz cherry tomatoes
90 g/3^1/$_4$ oz low-fat cream
    cheese
1 tsp runny honey
pinch of smoked paprika
1 tsp chopped fresh parsley

marinade

1 tsp vegetable oil
1 tsp fresh rosemary
1 tbsp fresh lemon thyme
1 tbsp lemon juice
4 tbsp white wine
1 tsp sugar
2 tbsp chopped fresh basil
^{1}/$_4$ tsp smoked paprika

method

1 Bake the potatoes in a preheated oven, 200°C/400°F/Gas Mark 6, for 30 minutes, then remove and cut into wedges – the flesh should not be completely cooked.

2 To make the marinade, finely chop the rosemary and lemon thyme, then place all the ingredients in a bowl and blend with a hand-held electric blender until smooth, or use a food processor.

3 Put the potato wedges into a large bowl with the aubergine, onion, peppers and courgettes, then pour over the marinade and mix thoroughly.

4 Arrange the vegetables on a non-stick baking sheet and roast in the oven, turning occasionally, for 25–30 minutes, or until golden brown and tender. Add the tomatoes for the last 5 minutes of the cooking time, just to split the skins and warm slightly.

5 Mix the cream cheese, honey and paprika together in a bowl.

6 Serve the vegetables with the cream cheese mixture and sprinkled with chopped parsley.

courgette & cheese gratin

ingredients

SERVES 4–6

55 g/2 oz unsalted butter

6 courgettes, sliced

salt and pepper

2 tbsp chopped fresh
    tarragon or a mixture of
    mint, tarragon and
    flat-leaf parsley

200 g/7 oz Gruyère or
    Parmesan cheese, grated

125 ml/4fl oz milk

125 ml/4fl oz double cream

2 eggs

freshly grated nutmeg

method

1 Melt the butter in a large sauté pan or frying pan over medium–high heat. Add the courgettes and sauté for 4–6 minutes, turning the slices over occasionally, until coloured on both sides. Remove from the pan and drain on kitchen paper, then season to taste with salt and pepper.

2 Spread half the courgettes over the bottom of a greased ovenproof serving dish. Sprinkle with half the herbs and 55 g/2 oz of the cheese. Repeat these layers once more.

3 Mix the milk, cream and eggs together and add nutmeg, salt and pepper. Pour this liquid over the courgettes, then sprinkle the top with the remaining cheese.

4 Bake in a preheated oven, 180°C/350°F/Gas Mark 4, for 35–45 minutes, or until it is set in the centre and golden brown. Remove from the oven and let stand for 5 minutes before serving straight from the dish.

cherry tomato clafoutis

ingredients

SERVES 4–6

400 g/14 oz cherry tomatoes

3 tbsp chopped fresh flat-leaf
    parsley, snipped fresh
    chives, or finely shredded
    fresh basil

100 g/3$\frac{1}{2}$ oz grated Gruyère
    cheese

55 g/2 oz plain flour

4 large eggs, lightly beaten

3 tbsp sour cream

225 ml/8 fl oz milk

salt and pepper

method

1 Lightly grease an oval ovenproof dish. Arrange the cherry tomatoes in the dish and sprinkle with the herbs and half the cheese.

2 Put the flour in a mixing bowl, then slowly add the eggs, whisking until smooth. Whisk in the sour cream, then slowly whisk in the milk to make a thin, smooth batter. Season with salt and pepper.

3 Gently pour the batter over the tomatoes, then sprinkle the top with the remaining cheese. Bake in a preheated oven, 190°C/ 375°F/Gas Mark 5, for 40–45 minutes, or until set and puffy, covering the top with foil if it browns too much before the batter sets. If serving hot, cool the clafoutis for a few minutes before cutting, or cool to room temperature.

caramelized onion tart

ingredients

SERVES 4–6

7 tbsp unsalted butter

600 g/1 lb 5 oz onions,
    thinly sliced

2 eggs

100 ml/3^1/$_2$ fl oz double
    cream

salt and pepper

100 g/3^1/$_2$ oz grated Gruyère
    cheese

20-cm/8-inch ready-baked
    pastry case

100 g/3^1/$_2$ oz coarsely grated
    Parmesan cheese

method

1 Melt the butter in a heavy-based frying pan over medium heat. Add the onions and cook, stirring frequently to avoid burning, for 30 minutes, or until well-browned and caramelized. Remove the onions from the pan and set aside.

2 Beat the eggs in a large bowl, stir in the cream and season to taste with salt and pepper. Add the Gruyère and mix well. Stir in the cooked onions.

3 Pour the egg and onion mixture into the baked pastry case and sprinkle with the Parmesan cheese. Place on a baking sheet. Bake in a preheated oven, 190°C/375°F/Gas Mark 5, for 15–20 minutes until the filling has set and begun to brown.

4 Remove from the oven and let rest for at least 10 minutes. The tart can be served hot or left to cool to room temperature.

broccoli & sesame frittata

ingredients

SERVES 2

175 g/6 oz broccoli, broken
into small florets

85 g/3 oz asparagus spears,
sliced diagonally

1 tbsp virgin olive oil

1 onion, cut into small wedges

2–4 garlic cloves, finely
chopped

1 large orange pepper,
deseeded and chopped

4 eggs

3 tbsp cold water

salt and pepper

25 g/1 oz sesame seeds

15 g/^{1}/$_2$ oz freshly grated
Parmesan cheese

3 spring onions, finely sliced

method

1 Cook the broccoli in a saucepan of lightly salted boiling water for 4 minutes. Add the asparagus after 2 minutes. Drain, then plunge into cold water. Drain again and set aside.

2 Heat the oil in a large frying pan over low heat, add the onion, garlic and orange pepper and cook, stirring frequently, for 8 minutes, or until the vegetables have softened.

3 Beat the eggs with the water, salt and pepper in a medium-size bowl. Pour into the frying pan, add the broccoli and asparagus and stir gently. Cook over medium heat for 3–4 minutes, drawing the mixture from the edges of the pan into the centre, allowing the uncooked egg to flow to the edges of the pan. Preheat the grill.

4 Sprinkle the top of the frittata with the sesame seeds and cheese and cook under the preheated grill for 3–5 minutes, or until golden and set. Sprinkle with the spring onions, cut into wedges and serve. Serve warm or cold.

baked eggs with cream, spinach & parmesan

ingredients

SERVES 2

2 tbsp butter, plus extra
   for greasing
125 g/4¹/₂ oz baby spinach
¹/₂ tsp freshly grated nutmeg
4 small eggs
50 ml/2 fl oz single cream
2 tbsp freshly grated
   Parmesan cheese
salt and pepper

method

1 Lightly grease 2 individual ceramic gratin dishes, or similar.

2 Melt the butter in a large frying pan over low heat and add the spinach. Cook for 1 minute, stirring with a wooden spoon until the spinach starts to wilt. Season with a little nutmeg, then divide between the prepared dishes.

3 Gently break 2 eggs into each dish. Pour the cream over them and sprinkle with grated Parmesan, then season with salt and pepper. Bake in a preheated oven, 160°C/325°F/Gas Mark 2¹/₂, for 10 minutes, or until the whites of the eggs have set but the yolks remain runny. Serve at once.

mushroom stroganoff

ingredients

SERVES 4

550 g/1 lb 4 oz mixed fresh
  mushrooms, such as
  chestnut, chanterelles,
  cèpes and oyster

1 red onion, diced

2 garlic cloves, crushed

425 ml/15 fl oz vegetable
  stock

1 tbsp tomato paste

2 tbsp lemon juice

scant 1 tbsp cornflour

2 tbsp cold water

115 g/4 oz low-fat
  plain yogurt

3 tbsp chopped fresh parsley

pepper

boiled brown or white rice
  and crisp green salad,
  to serve

method

1 Put the mushrooms, onion, garlic, stock, tomato paste and lemon juice into a saucepan and bring to the boil. Reduce the heat, cover and simmer for 15 minutes, or until the onion is tender.

2 Blend the cornflour with the water in a small bowl and stir into the mushroom mixture. Return to the boil, stirring constantly, and cook until the sauce thickens. Reduce the heat and simmer for a further 2–3 minutes, stirring occasionally.

3 Just before serving, remove the pan from the heat, and stir in the yogurt, making sure that the stroganoff is not boiling or it may separate and curdle. Stir in 2 tablespoons of the parsley and season with pepper. Transfer the stroganoff to a warmed serving dish, sprinkle over the remaining parsley and serve at once with boiled brown or white rice and a crisp green salad.

vegetable & coconut curry

ingredients

SERVES 4

1 onion, coarsely chopped

3 garlic cloves, thinly sliced

2.5-cm/1-inch piece fresh
    root ginger, thinly sliced

2 fresh green chillies,
    deseeded and finely
    chopped

1 tbsp vegetable oil

1 tsp ground turmeric

1 tsp ground coriander

1 tsp ground cumin

1 kg/2 lb 4 oz mixed
    vegetables, such as
    cauliflower, courgettes,
    potatoes, carrots and
    green beans, cut into
    chunks

200 g/7 oz coconut cream
    or milk

salt and pepper

2 tbsp chopped fresh
    coriander, to garnish

freshly cooked rice, to serve

method

1 Put the onion, garlic, ginger and chillies in a food processor and process until almost smooth.

2 Heat the oil in a large, heavy-based pan over medium-low heat, add the onion mixture and cook, stirring constantly, for 5 minutes.

3 Add the turmeric, coriander and cumin and cook, stirring frequently, for 3–4 minutes. Add the vegetables and stir well to coat in the spice paste.

4 Add the coconut cream or milk to the vegetables, cover and simmer for 30–40 minutes until the vegetables are tender.

5 Season with salt and pepper, garnish with the chopped coriander and serve with rice.

Thai yellow vegetable curry with brown basmati rice

ingredients

SERVES 4

50 g/1³/4 oz yellow pepper, deseeded

50 g/1³/4 oz celery

50 g/1³/4 oz baby corn

85 g/3 oz leek

100 g/3¹/2 oz sweet potato

100 g/3¹/2 oz pak choi

50 g/1³/4 oz courgette

50 g/1³/4 oz mangetout

300 ml/10 fl oz pineapple juice

200 ml/7 fl oz water

3 tbsp lime juice

2 tbsp cornflour

4 tbsp low-fat plain yogurt

4 tbsp chopped fresh coriander

150 g/5¹/2 oz cooked brown basmati rice

spice mix

1 tsp finely chopped garlic

¹/4 tsp ground turmeric

1 tsp ground coriander

1 tsp finely chopped lemongrass

3 kaffir lime leaves

1 tsp finely chopped green chilli

method

1 To make the spice mix, pound all the spices to a fine paste using a mortar and pestle.

2 To prepare the vegetables, cut the yellow pepper into 1-cm/¹/2-inch squares, cut the celery, baby corn and leek into 5-mm/¹/4-inch lengths, and cut the sweet potato into 1-cm/¹/2-inch cubes. Shred the pak choi. Cut the courgette into 5-mm/¹/4-inch cubes and slice the mangetout into thin strips.

3 Put the pepper, celery, baby corn, leek, sweet potato, pineapple juice, water and the spice mix into a large saucepan with a lid and bring to the boil. Reduce the heat and skim the scum from the surface with a metal spoon. Cover and simmer for 15 minutes.

4 Add the pak choi, courgette and mangetout and cook for 2 minutes. Add the lime juice, then gradually add the cornflour blended with a little cold water. Cook, stirring constantly, until thickened to the required consistency.

5 Remove the curry from the heat and cool for 2–3 minutes. Stir in the yogurt. (Do not boil once the yogurt has been added or the curry will separate.) Stir in the fresh coriander and serve the curry with the rice.

roasted garlic
mashed potatoes

ingredients

SERVES 4

2 whole garlic bulbs
1 tbsp olive oil
900 g/2 lb floury potatoes,
    peeled
125 ml/4 fl oz milk
55 g/2 oz butter
salt and pepper

method

1 Separate the garlic cloves, place on a large piece of foil and drizzle with the oil. Wrap the garlic in the foil and roast in a preheated oven, 180°C/350°F/Gas Mark 4, for about 1 hour, or until very tender. Let cool slightly.

2 Meanwhile, cut the potatoes into chunks, then cook in a saucepan of lightly salted boiling water for 15 minutes, or until tender.

3 Squeeze the cooled garlic cloves out of their skins and push through a sieve into a saucepan. Add the milk and butter and season with salt and pepper. Heat gently until the butter has melted.

4 Drain the cooked potatoes, then mash in the pan until smooth. Pour in the garlic mixture and heat gently, stirring, until the ingredients are combined. Serve hot.

roasted squash wedges

ingredients

SERVES 4

200 g/7 oz butternut squash
    or other type of squash,
    peeled, deseeded and cut
    into 4 wedges

1 tsp vegetable oil

100 g/3$^1/_2$ oz onion,
    finely chopped

1 tsp minced garlic

70 g/2$^1/_2$ oz three-grain risotto
    mix (baldo rice, spelt and
    pearl barley – this is
    available ready-mixed)

300 ml/10 fl oz vegetable
    stock

225 g/8 oz asparagus tips

2 tbsp finely chopped fresh
    marjoram, plus extra
    to garnish

3 tbsp low-fat cream cheese

2 tbsp finely chopped
    fresh parsley

pepper

method

1 Spread out the squash wedges on a non-stick baking sheet and roast in a preheated oven, 200°C/400°F/Gas Mark 6, for 20 minutes, or until tender and golden brown.

2 Meanwhile, heat the oil in a medium saucepan over high heat, add the onion and garlic and cook, stirring, until softened but not coloured. Add the risotto mix and stir in half the stock. Simmer, stirring occasionally, until the stock has reduced in the pan. Pour in the remaining stock and continue to cook, stirring occasionally, until the grains are tender.

3 Cut 175 g/6 oz of the asparagus into 10-cm/4-inch lengths and blanch in a saucepan of boiling water for 2 minutes. Drain and keep warm. Cut the remaining asparagus into 5-mm/$^1/4$-inch slices and add to the risotto for the last 3 minutes of the cooking time.

4 Remove the risotto from the heat and stir in the marjoram, cream cheese and parsley. Season with pepper. Do not reboil.

5 To serve, lay the squash wedges on warmed serving plates, then spoon over the risotto and top with the asparagus. Garnish with marjoram.

stir-fried broccoli

ingredients

SERVES 4

2 tbsp vegetable oil

2 broccoli heads,
    cut into florets

2 tbsp soy sauce

1 tsp cornflour

1 tbsp caster sugar

1 tsp grated fresh root ginger

1 garlic clove, crushed

pinch of dried red pepper flakes

1 tsp toasted sesame seeds,
    to garnish

method

1 Heat the oil in a large preheated wok or skillet over high heat until almost smoking. Add the broccoli and stir-fry for 4–5 minutes. Reduce the heat to medium.

2 Combine the soy sauce, cornflour, sugar, ginger, garlic and red pepper flakes in a small bowl. Add the mixture to the broccoli and cook, stirring constantly, for 2–3 minutes until the sauce thickens slightly.

3 Transfer to a warmed serving dish, garnish with the sesame seeds and serve immediately.

roasted onions

ingredients

SERVES 4

8 large onions, peeled
3 tbsp olive oil
55 g/2 oz butter
2 tsp chopped fresh thyme
salt and pepper
200 g/7 oz Cheddar cheese,
    grated

method

1 Cut a cross down through the top of the onions towards the root, without cutting all the way through. Place the onions in a roasting pan and drizzle over the olive oil.

2 Press a little of the butter into the open crosses, sprinkle with the thyme and season with salt and pepper. Cover with foil and roast in a preheated oven, 180°C/350°F/Gas Mark 4, for 40–45 minutes.

3 Remove from the oven, take off the foil and baste the onions with the pan juices. Return to the oven and cook for a further 15 minutes, uncovered, to allow the onions to brown.

4 Take the onions out of the oven and scatter the grated cheese over them. Return them to the oven for a few minutes so that the cheese starts to melt. Serve immediately.

brussels sprouts
with chestnuts

ingredients

SERVES 4

450 g/1 lb Brussels sprouts

115 g/4 oz unsalted butter

55 g/2 oz brown sugar

115 g/4 oz cooked and
    peeled chestnuts

method

1 Trim the Brussels sprouts and remove and discard any loose outer leaves. Add to a large saucepan of boiling salted water and boil for 5–10 minutes until just tender, but not too soft. Drain well, refresh under cold water and drain again. Set aside.

2 Melt the butter in a heavy-based frying pan over medium heat. Add the sugar and stir until dissolved. Add the chestnuts and cook, stirring occasionally, until well coated and beginning to brown.

3 Add the sprouts to the chestnuts and mix well. Reduce the heat and cook gently, stirring occasionally, for 3–4 minutes to heat through.

4 Remove from the heat, transfer to a warmed serving dish and serve immediately.

tabbouleh

ingredients

SERVES 4

175 g/6 oz bulgur wheat

3 tbsp extra-virgin olive oil

4 tbsp lemon juice

salt and pepper

4 spring onions

1 green pepper, deseeded
    and sliced

4 tomatoes, chopped

2 tbsp chopped fresh parsley

2 tbsp chopped fresh mint

8 black olives, pitted

method

1 Place the bulgur wheat in a large bowl and add enough cold water to cover. Let stand for 30 minutes, or until the wheat has doubled in size. Drain well and press out as much liquid as possible. Spread out the wheat on paper towels to dry.

2 Place the wheat in a serving bowl. Mix the olive oil and lemon juice together in a jug and season to taste with salt and pepper. Pour the lemon mixture over the wheat and marinate for 1 hour.

3 Using a sharp knife, finely chop the spring onions, then add to the salad with the green pepper, tomatoes, parsley and mint and toss lightly to mix. Top the salad with the olives and serve immediately.

papaya, avocado & red pepper salad

ingredients

SERVES 4–6

200 g/7 oz mixed salad leaves

2–3 spring onions, chopped

3–4 tbsp chopped fresh
   coriander

1 small papaya

2 red peppers

1 avocado

1 tbsp lime juice

3–4 tbsp pumpkin seeds,
   preferably toasted (optional)

dressing

juice of 1 lime

large pinch of paprika

large pinch of ground cumin

large pinch of sugar

1 garlic clove, finely chopped

4 tbsp extra-virgin olive oil

salt

dash of white wine vinegar
   (optional)

method

1 Combine the salad leaves with the spring onions and coriander in a bowl. Mix well, then transfer the salad to a large serving dish.

2 Cut the papaya in half and scoop out the seeds with a spoon. Cut into quarters, remove the peel and slice the flesh. Arrange on top of the salad leaves. Cut the peppers in half, remove the cores and seeds, then thinly slice. Add the peppers to the salad leaves.

3 Cut the avocado in half around the stone. Twist apart, then remove the stone with a knife. Carefully peel off the skin, dice the flesh and toss in lime juice to prevent discoloration. Add to the other salad ingredients.

4 To make the dressing, whisk the lime juice, paprika, cumin, sugar, garlic and oil together in a small bowl. Season with salt.

5 Pour the dressing over the salad and toss lightly, adding a dash of wine vinegar if a flavour with more 'bite' is preferred. Sprinkle with pumpkin seeds, if using.

avocado salad
with lime dressing

ingredients

SERVES 4

60 g/2¼ oz mixed red and
    green lettuce leaves

60 g/2¼ oz wild rocket

4 spring onions, finely diced

5 tomatoes, sliced

25 g/1 oz walnuts, toasted
    and chopped

2 avocados

1 tbsp lemon juice

lime dressing

1 tbsp lime juice

1 tsp French mustard

1 tbsp sour cream

1 tbsp chopped fresh parsley
    or coriander

3 tbsp extra-virgin olive oil

pinch of sugar

salt and pepper

method

1 Wash and drain the lettuce and rocket, if
necessary. Shred all the leaves and arrange
in the bottom of a large salad bowl. Add the
spring onions, tomatoes and walnuts.

2 Stone, peel and thinly slice or dice the
avocados. Brush with the lemon juice to
prevent discoloration, then transfer to the
salad bowl. Gently mix together.

3 To make the dressing, put all the dressing
ingredients in a screw-top jar and shake well.
Drizzle over the salad and serve immediately.

roasted pepper salad

ingredients

SERVES 8

3 red peppers

3 yellow peppers

5 tbsp Spanish extra-virgin
   olive oil

2 tbsp dry sherry vinegar or
   lemon juice

2 garlic cloves, crushed

pinch of sugar

salt and pepper

1 tbsp capers

8 small black Spanish olives

2 tbsp chopped fresh
   marjoram, plus extra
   sprigs to garnish

method

1 Preheat the grill to high. Place the peppers on a wire rack or grill pan and cook under the grill for 10 minutes, until their skins have blackened and blistered, turning them frequently.

2 Remove the roasted peppers from the heat, and either put them in a bowl and immediately cover tightly with a clean, damp tea towel or put them in a plastic bag. The steam helps to soften the skins and makes it easier to remove them. Let stand for about 15 minutes, until cool enough to handle.

3 Holding one pepper at a time over a clean bowl, use a sharp knife to make a small hole in the base and gently squeeze out the juices and reserve them. Still holding the pepper over the bowl, carefully peel off the blackened skin with your fingers, or a knife, and discard it. Cut the peppers in half and remove the stem, core and seeds, then cut each pepper into neat thin strips. Arrange the pepper strips on a serving dish.

4 To the reserved pepper juices add the olive oil, sherry vinegar, garlic, sugar, salt and pepper. Whisk together until combined. Drizzle the dressing evenly over the salad.

5 Sprinkle the capers, olives and chopped marjoram over the salad, garnish with marjoram sprigs and serve at room temperature.

green bean salad with feta cheese

ingredients

SERVES 4

350 g/12 oz green beans

1 red onion, chopped

3–4 tbsp chopped fresh
    coriander

2 radishes, thinly sliced

75 g/2¾ oz feta cheese
    drained weight, crumbled

1 tsp chopped fresh oregano,
    plus extra leaves to garnish
    (optional), or ½ tsp dried

pepper

2 tbsp red wine or fruit vinegar

80 ml/3 fl oz extra-virgin olive
    oil

3 ripe tomatoes, cut into
    wedges

slices of crusty bread,
    to serve

method

1 Bring about 5 cm/2 inches of water to the boil in the bottom of a steamer. Add the beans to the top part of the steamer, cover and steam for 5 minutes, or until just tender.

2 Place the beans in a large bowl and add the onion, coriander, radishes and feta cheese.

3 Sprinkle the oregano over the salad, then season with pepper. Mix the vinegar and oil together in a small bowl and pour over the salad. Toss gently to mix well.

4 Transfer to a serving platter, surround with the tomato wedges and serve at once with slices of crusty bread, or cover and chill until ready to serve.

greek salad

ingredients

SERVES 4

4 tomatoes, cut into wedges

1 onion, sliced

1/2 cucumber, sliced

225 g/8 oz kalamata olives,
    stoned

225 g/8 oz feta cheese,
    cubed

2 tbsp fresh coriander leaves

fresh flat-leaf parsley sprigs,
    to garnish

pitta bread, to serve

dressing

5 tbsp extra-virgin olive oil

2 tbsp white wine vinegar

1 tbsp lemon juice

1/2 tsp sugar

1 tbsp chopped fresh
    coriander

salt and pepper

method

1 To make the dressing, put all the ingredients for the dressing into a large bowl and mix well together.

2 Add the tomatoes, onion, cucumber, olives, cheese and coriander. Toss all the ingredients together, then divide between individual serving bowls. Garnish with parsley sprigs and serve with pitta bread.

desserts

Vegetarians usually take a great interest in the nutritional content of their food and have often chosen this lifestyle with a view to becoming healthier and remaining that way. This does not mean, however, that vegetarians do not enjoy an occasional dessert!

This chapter has a mix of dessert recipes, some of which are health-conscious and some of which are completely indulgent for those days when nothing less will do. If you follow a low-fat diet, choose the Icy Fruit Blizzard, Apricot & Passion Fruit Sorbet or the Blueberry Frozen Yogurt, which is also a treat for diabetics. The Baked Apricots with Honey, Blueberry Filo Tart and Spiced Baked Goat's Yogurt are also low-fat.

If you want to relax just a little, try the Raspberry Ripple Ice Cream, Lemon Yogurt Ice Cream, Creamy Mango Brûlée, Mascarpone Creams, Creamy Chocolate Pudding or the Summer Pudding.

And if you want to go completely wild? Well, three obvious choices are the Banoffee Pies, the Mississippi Mud Pie and the Chocolate Fudge Tart. Spanish Caramel Custard will also fit the bill, and if you want to be really naughty, make the Rich Vanilla Ice Cream and serve it with home-made Apple Pie – two in one!

raspberry ripple ice cream

ingredients

SERVES 6

85 g/3 oz fresh or frozen
   raspberries, thawed if
   frozen, plus extra to serve
2 tbsp water
2 eggs
1 tbsp caster sugar
300 ml/10 fl oz milk, warmed
1 tsp vanilla essence
300 ml/10 fl oz double cream

method

1 Turn the freezer to rapid. Put the raspberries into a saucepan with the water and bring to the boil, then reduce the heat and simmer gently for 5 minutes. Remove from the heat and cool for 30 minutes. Transfer to a food processor or blender and process to a purée, then rub through a nylon sieve to remove the pips. Set aside.

2 Beat the eggs in a bowl. Stir the sugar into the warmed milk, then slowly pour onto the eggs, beating constantly. Strain into a clean saucepan and cook over low heat, stirring constantly, for 8–10 minutes, or until the custard thickens and coats the back of a wooden spoon. Add the vanilla essence, remove from the heat and let cool.

3 Half-whip the cream in a large bowl, then slowly stir in the cooled custard. Pour into a freezerproof container and freeze for 1 1/2 hours, or until starting to set around the outside. Remove from the freezer and stir the mixture, breaking up any ice crystals.

4 Return the mixture to the freezer and freeze for a further hour, then remove from the freezer again and gently stir in the raspberry purée to give a rippled effect. Return to the freezer for a further hour or until frozen. Serve in scoops with extra fresh raspberries.

rich vanilla ice cream

ingredients

SERVES 4–6

300 ml/10 fl oz single cream
and 300 ml/10 fl oz
double cream or 625ml/
20 fl oz whipping cream

1 vanilla bean

4 large egg yolks

100 g/3^1/$_2$ oz caster sugar

method

1 Pour the single and double cream or whipping cream into a large heavy-based saucepan. Split open the vanilla bean and scrape out the seeds into the cream, then add the whole vanilla bean too. Bring almost to the boil, then remove from the heat and infuse for 30 minutes.

2 Put the egg yolks and sugar in a large bowl and whisk together until pale and the mixture leaves a trail when the whisk is lifted. Remove the vanilla bean from the cream, then slowly add the cream to the egg mixture, stirring all the time with a wooden spoon. Strain the mixture into the rinsed-out pan or a double boiler and cook over low heat for 10–15 minutes, stirring all the time, until the mixture thickens enough to coat the back of the spoon. Do not let the mixture boil or it will curdle. Remove the custard from the heat and cool for at least 1 hour, stirring from time to time to prevent a skin forming.

3 Churn the custard in an ice-cream maker following the manufacturer's instructions. Serve immediately if wished, or transfer to a freezerproof container, cover with a lid and store in the freezer.

lemon yogurt ice cream

ingredients

SERVES 4–6

2–3 lemons

625 ml/20 fl oz Greek-style yogurt

150 ml/5 fl oz double cream

100 g/3½ oz caster sugar

finely pared orange rind, to garnish

method

1 Squeeze the juice from the lemons – you need 6 tablespoons in total. Put the juice into a bowl, add the yogurt, cream and sugar, and mix well together.

2 If using an ice-cream machine, churn the mixture in the machine following the manufacturer's instructions. Alternatively, freeze the mixture in a freezerproof container, uncovered, for 1–2 hours, or until it starts to set around the edges. Turn the mixture into a bowl and stir with a fork or beat in a food processor until smooth. Return to the freezer and freeze for a further 2–3 hours, or until firm or required. Cover the container with a lid for storing. Serve with finely pared orange rind.

icy fruit blizzard

ingredients

SERVES 4

1 pineapple

1 large piece seeded
    watermelon, peeled and
    cut into small pieces

225 g/8 oz strawberries or
    other berries, hulled and
    left whole or sliced

1 mango, peach or nectarine,
    peeled and sliced

1 banana, peeled and sliced

orange juice

caster sugar, to taste

method

1 Cover 2 non-stick baking sheets or ordinary baking sheets with a sheet of clingfilm. Arrange the fruits on top and open freeze for at least 2 hours, or until firm and icy.

2 Place one type of fruit in a food processor and process until it is all broken up into small pieces.

3 Add a little orange juice and sugar to taste, and continue to process until it forms a granular mixture. Repeat with the remaining fruits. Arrange in chilled bowls and serve immediately.

blueberry frozen yogurt

ingredients

SERVES 4

175 g/6 oz fresh blueberries

finely grated rind and
  juice of 1 orange

3 tbsp maple syrup

500 g/1 lb 2 oz plain
  low-fat yogurt

method

1 Put the blueberries and orange juice into a food processor or blender and process to a purée. Strain through a nylon sieve into a bowl or jug.

2 Stir the maple syrup and yogurt together in a large mixing bowl, then fold in the fruit purée.

3 Churn the mixture in an ice-cream machine, following the manufacturer's instructions, then freeze for 5–6 hours. If you don't have an ice-cream machine, transfer the mixture to a freezerproof container, and freeze for 2 hours. Remove from the freezer, turn out into a bowl and beat until smooth. Return to the freezer and freeze until firm.

apricot & passion fruit sorbet

ingredients

SERVES 6

sorbet

100 g/3½ oz no-soak dried
    apricots

250 ml/9 fl oz water

2 tbsp freshly squeezed
    lemon juice

2 tbsp freshly squeezed
    orange juice

7 tbsp passion fruit pulp,
    sieved to remove
    the seeds

sesame snaps

1 tbsp sesame seeds

1 tbsp liquid glucose

3 tbsp caster sugar

2 tbsp plain flour

method

1 To make the sorbet, put the apricots in a saucepan with the water and bring to the boil. Reduce the heat and simmer for 10–15 minutes, or until soft. Remove from the heat. Purée the apricots in a food processor with the water, then blend in the lemon juice, orange juice and 3 tablespoons of the passion fruit pulp.

2 Add 2 tablespoons of the passion fruit pulp, mix well, then transfer to a large, freezerproof container and freeze for 20 minutes. Beat the sorbet to break down the ice crystals, then return to the freezer for a further 2 hours, or until fully frozen, beating every 20 minutes to give a smooth texture to the finished sorbet.

3 To make the sesame snaps, toss the sesame seeds in a small saucepan over high heat until golden brown. Remove from the heat, add the glucose, sugar and flour and mix with a metal spoon to form a sticky paste. Remove from the pan and cool slightly. Roll the paste into a sausage shape and cut into 16 pieces. With wet hands, roll each piece into a small ball, then lightly press out onto a sheet of silicone.

4 Bake in a preheated oven, 180°C/350°F/Gas Mark 4, for 6 minutes until golden. Transfer to a wire rack and let cool. Serve the sorbet with the remaining passion fruit pulp spooned over and the sesame snaps to accompany.

spanish caramel custard

ingredients

SERVES 6

500 ml/18 fl oz whole milk

$^1/_2$ orange with 2 long, thin
    pieces of rind pared off
    and reserved

1 vanilla bean, split, or
    $^1/_2$ tsp vanilla essence

175 g/6 oz caster sugar

butter, for greasing the dish

3 large eggs, plus 2 large
    egg yolks

method

1 Pour the milk into a saucepan with the orange rind and vanilla bean or essence. Bring to the boil, then remove from the heat and stir in 85 g/3 oz of the sugar; set aside for at least 30 minutes to infuse.

2 Meanwhile, put the remaining sugar and 4 tablespoons of water in another saucepan over medium–high heat. Stir until the sugar dissolves, then boil without stirring until the caramel turns deep golden brown. Remove from the heat at once and squeeze in a few drops of orange juice to stop the cooking. Pour into a lightly buttered 1-litre/32-fl oz soufflé dish and swirl to cover the base; set aside.

3 Return the pan of infused milk to the heat, and bring to a simmer. Beat the whole eggs and egg yolks together in a heatproof bowl. Pour the warm milk into the eggs, whisking constantly. Strain into the soufflé dish.

4 Place the soufflé dish in a roasting pan and pour in enough boiling water to come halfway up the sides of the dish. Bake in a preheated oven, 160°C/325°F/Gas Mark 2$^1/_2$, for 75–90 minutes until set and a knife inserted in the centre comes out clean. Remove the dish from the roasting pan, set aside to cool, then cover and chill overnight. To serve, run a metal spatula round the dish, then invert onto a serving plate, shaking firmly to release.

creamy mango brûlée

ingredients

SERVES 4

2 mangoes

250 g/9 oz Mascarpone
  cheese

200 ml/7 fl oz Greek-style
  yogurt

1 tsp ground ginger

grated rind and juice of 1 lime

2 tbsp soft light brown sugar

8 tbsp raw brown sugar

method

1 Slice the mangoes on either side of the stone. Discard the stone and peel the fruit. Slice and then chop the fruit. Divide it between 4 ramekins.

2 Beat the Mascarpone cheese with the yogurt. Fold in the ginger, lime rind and juice and soft brown sugar. Divide the mixture between the ramekins and level off the tops. Chill for 2 hours.

3 Sprinkle 2 tablespoons of raw brown sugar over the top of each dish, covering the creamy mixture. Place under a hot grill for 2–3 minutes, until melted and browned. Let cool, then chill until needed. This dessert should be eaten on the day it is made.

mascarpone creams

ingredients

SERVES 4

115 g/4 oz Amaretti biscuits,
    crushed

4 tbsp Amaretto or
    Maraschino

4 eggs, separated

55 g/2 oz caster sugar

225 g/8 oz Mascarpone
    cheese

toasted flaked almonds,
    to decorate

method

1 Place the Amaretti crumbs in a bowl, add the Amaretto or Maraschino and set aside to soak.

2 Meanwhile, beat the egg yolks with the caster sugar until pale and thick. Fold in the Mascarpone and soaked biscuit crumbs.

3 Whisk the egg whites in a separate, spotlessly clean bowl until stiff, then gently fold into the cheese mixture. Divide the Mascarpone cream between 4 serving dishes and chill for 1–2 hours. Sprinkle with toasted slivered almonds just before serving.

creamy chocolate pudding

ingredients

SERVES 4–6

175 g/6 oz plain chocolate, at
    least 70% cocoa solids,
    broken up
1¹/₂ tbsp orange juice
3 tbsp water
2 tbsp unsalted butter, diced
2 eggs, separated
¹/₈ tsp cream of tartar
3 tbsp caster sugar
6 tbsp double cream
orange wedges, to serve

pistachio-orange
praline
corn oil, for greasing
55 g/2 oz caster sugar
55 g/2 oz shelled pistachios
finely grated rind of
    1 large orange

method

1 Melt the chocolate with the orange juice and
water in a small saucepan over very low heat,
stirring constantly. Remove from the heat and
melt in the butter until incorporated. Using a
rubber spatula, scrape the chocolate into a
bowl. Beat the egg yolks until blended, then
beat them into the chocolate mixture. Set aside
to cool.

2 In a clean bowl, whisk the egg whites with
the cream of tartar until soft peaks form. Beat
in the sugar, 1 tablespoon at a time, beating
well after each addition, until the meringue is
glossy. Beat 1 tablespoon of the meringue
into the chocolate mixture, then fold in the rest.

3 In a separate bowl, whip the cream until soft
peaks form. Fold into the chocolate mixture.
Spoon into individual glass bowls or wine
glasses or 1 large serving bowl. Cover with
clingfilm and chill for at least 4 hours.

4 To make the praline, lightly grease a baking
sheet with corn oil and set aside. Put the
sugar and pistachios in a small saucepan over
medium heat. When the sugar starts to melt,
stir gently until a liquid caramel forms and the
nuts start popping. Pour the praline onto the
baking sheet and immediately finely grate the
orange rind over. Cool until firm then coarsely
chop. Just before serving, sprinkle the praline
over the chocolate pudding and serve with
orange wedges.

summer pudding

ingredients

SERVES 6

675 g/1 lb 8 oz mixed soft
    fruits, such as redcurrants,
    blackcurrants, raspberries
    and blackberries

140 g/5 oz caster sugar

2 tbsp crème de framboise
    liqueur (optional)

6–8 slices of good day-old
    white bread, crusts removed

double cream, to serve

method

1 Place the fruits in a large saucepan with the sugar. Over low heat, very slowly bring to the boil, stirring carefully to ensure that the sugar has dissolved. Cook over low heat for only 2–3 minutes, until the juices run but the fruit still holds its shape. Add the liqueur if using.

2 Line an 875-ml/28-fl oz pudding bowl with some of the slices of bread (cut them to shape so that the bread fits well). Spoon in the cooked fruit and juices, reserving a little of the juice for later.

3 Cover the surface of the fruit with the remaining bread. Place a plate on top of the pudding and weight it down for at least 8 hours or overnight in the refrigerator.

4 Turn out the pudding and pour over the reserved juices to colour any white bits of bread that may still be showing. Serve with the double cream.

baked apricots with honey

ingredients

SERVES 4

butter, for greasing

4 apricots, each cut in half
    and pitted

4 tbsp flaked almonds

4 tbsp honey

pinch ground ginger or grated
    nutmeg

method

1 Lightly butter an ovenproof dish large enough to hold the apricot halves in a single layer.

2 Arrange the apricot halves in the dish, cut side up. Sprinkle with the almonds and drizzle the honey over. Dust with the spice.

3 Bake in a preheated oven, 200°C/400°F/Gas Mark 6, for 12–15 minutes until the apricots are tender and the almonds golden. Remove from the oven and serve at once.

creamy rice pudding

ingredients

SERVES 4

1 tbsp butter, for greasing

85 g/3 oz sultanas

5 tbsp caster sugar

90 g/3¼ oz pudding rice

1.25 litres/40 fl oz milk

1 tsp vanilla essence

finely grated rind of 1 large
    lemon

pinch of nutmeg

chopped pistachios,
    to decorate

method

1 Grease an 875-ml/28-fl oz ovenproof dish with the butter.

2 Put the sultanas, sugar and rice into a mixing bowl, then stir in the milk and vanilla essence. Transfer to the greased ovenproof dish, sprinkle over the grated lemon rind and the nutmeg, then bake in a preheated oven, 160°C/325°F/Gas Mark 2½, for 2½ hours.

3 Remove from the oven and transfer to individual serving bowls. Decorate with chopped pistachios and serve.

banoffee pies

ingredients

SERVES 4

two cans sweetened
    condensed milk, about
    400 ml/14 fl oz each
6 tbsp butter, melted
150 g/5½ oz digestive biscuits,
    crushed into crumbs
50 g/1¾ oz almonds, toasted
    and ground
50 g/1¾ oz hazelnuts,
    toasted and ground
4 ripe bananas
1 tbsp lemon juice
1 tsp vanilla essence
75 g/2¾ oz chocolate flakes
450 ml/16 fl oz thick double
    cream, whipped

method

1 Place the cans of milk in a large saucepan and cover them with water. Bring to the boil, then reduce the heat and simmer for 2 hours, topping up the water level regularly to keep the cans covered. Carefully lift out the hot cans and set aside to cool.

2 Grease 4 individual loose-based tartlet pans with butter. Put the remaining butter into a bowl and add the biscuit crumbs and nuts. Mix together well, then press the mixture evenly into the bottom of the tartlet pans. Bake in a preheated oven, 180°C/350°F/Gas Mark 4, for 10–12 minutes, then remove from the oven and cool.

3 Open the cans of condensed milk and spread the contents over the biscuit base in the tartlet pans. Peel and slice the bananas and put them into a bowl. Sprinkle over the lemon juice and vanilla essence and mix gently. Spoon the banana mixture onto the condensed milk layer, then top with a dollop of whipped cream. Break up the chocolate flakes, scatter over the tartlets and serve.

blueberry filo tart

ingredients

SERVES 2

4 sheets of filo pastry

rapeseed or vegetable oil spray

200 g/7 oz Mascarpone cheese

1 tsp honey

1 tbsp finely grated
    lemon rind

3 tbsp lemon juice

1 tsp caster sugar

100 g/3^1/2 oz fresh blueberries

method

1 Using a plate as a guide, cut out 4 x 14-cm/5^1/2-inch circles of filo pastry (you need two circles per tartlet). Spray each lightly with oil before laying two circles into 2 x 10-cm/4-inch fluted tartlet pans, pressing the pastry into the corners. Prick the bases with a fork.

2 Put a ramekin into the centre of each tartlet shell to prevent the pastry rising, then bake in a preheated oven, 180°C/350°F/Gas Mark 4, for 5 minutes. Remove the ramekins and bake the cases for a further 4–5 minutes so that the bases cook. Remove from the oven and leave the shells to cool in the tins. Store in an airtight tin so that they remain crisp.

3 Mix the Mascarpone cheese with the honey in a small bowl.

4 Put the lemon rind and juice and the sugar in a small saucepan over low heat and heat until the liquid has evaporated, then add the blueberries. Stir with a metal spoon to coat the berries in the syrup. Remove from the heat and keep warm.

5 To serve, place each tartlet shell on a serving plate, add a spoonful of the Mascarpone mixture, then spoon over the warmed blueberries.

mississippi mud pie

ingredients

SERVES 8

pastry

250 g/9 oz plain flour, plus
  extra for dusting

2 tbsp cocoa powder

140 g/5 oz butter

2 tbsp caster sugar

1–2 tbsp cold water

filling

175 g/6 oz butter

250 g/9 oz packed brown
  sugar

4 eggs, lightly beaten

4 tbsp cocoa powder, sifted

150 g/5$^{1}/_{2}$ oz plain chocolate

300 ml/10 fl oz single cream

1 tsp chocolate extract

425 ml/15 fl oz whipped
  double cream and
  chocolate flakes and curls,
  to decorate

method

1 To make the pastry, sift the flour and cocoa into a mixing bowl. Rub in the butter with your fingertips until the mixture resembles fine breadcrumbs. Stir in the sugar and enough cold water to mix to a soft dough. Wrap the dough in clingfilm and chill in the refrigerator for 15 minutes.

2 Roll out the dough on a lightly floured work surface and use to line a 23-cm/9-inch loose-based tart pan or ceramic pie dish. Line with baking parchment and fill with dried beans. Bake in a preheated oven, 190°C/375°F/Gas Mark 5, for 15 minutes. Remove from the oven and take out the paper and beans. Bake the pastry case for a further 10 minutes.

3 To make the filling, beat the butter and sugar together in a bowl and gradually beat in the eggs, with the cocoa. Melt the chocolate and beat it into the mixture, with the single cream and the chocolate extract.

4 Reduce the oven temperature to 160°C/325°F/Gas Mark 2$^{1}/_{2}$. Pour the mixture into the pastry case and bake for 45 minutes, or until the filling has set gently. Let cool completely, then transfer to a serving plate.

5 Cover the mud pie with the whipped cream, decorate with chocolate flakes and curls and chill until ready to serve.

chestnut, maple syrup & pecan tart

ingredients

SERVES 6

pastry

115 g/4 oz plain flour

pinch of salt

75 g/2½ oz cold butter,
    cut into pieces

cold water

filling

1 kg/2 lb 4 oz canned
    sweetened chestnut purée

300 ml/10 fl oz double cream

2 tbsp butter

2 tbsp maple syrup

175 g/6 oz pecans

method

1 Lightly grease a 22-cm/9-inch loose-based fluted tart pan. Sift the flour and salt into a food processor, add the butter and process until the mixture resembles fine breadcrumbs. Tip the mixture into a large bowl and add a little cold water, just enough to bring the pastry together. Turn out onto a work surface dusted with more flour and roll out the pastry 8 cm/3¼ inches larger than the pan. Carefully lift the dough into the pan and press to fit. Roll the rolling pin over the pan to neaten the edges and trim the excess pastry. Fit a piece of baking parchment into the pastry case, fill with dried beans, and chill in the refrigerator for 30 minutes.

2 Remove from the refrigerator and bake in a preheated oven, 190°C/375°F/Gas Mark 5, for 15 minutes, then remove the beans and paper and bake for a further 10 minutes.

3 Empty the chestnut purée into a large bowl. Whip the cream until stiff and fold into the chestnut purée. Spoon into the cold pastry case and chill for 2 hours. Melt the butter with the maple syrup and when bubbling add the pecans and stir for 1–2 minutes. Spoon onto baking parchment and let cool. When ready to serve, arrange the pecans on the chestnut cream.

chocolate fudge tart

ingredients

SERVES 6–8

flour, for sprinkling

350 g/12 oz ready-made
    shortcrust pastry

icing sugar, for dusting

filling

140 g/5 oz plain chocolate,
    finely chopped

175 g/6 oz butter, diced

350 g/12 oz golden
    granulated sugar

100 g/3 1/2 oz plain flour

1/2 tsp vanilla essence

6 eggs, beaten

150 ml/5 fl oz whipped cream
    and ground cinnamon,
    to decorate

method

1 Roll out the pastry on a lightly floured work surface and use to line a 20-cm/8-inch deep loose-based tart pan. Prick the pastry base lightly with a fork, then line with foil and fill with baking beans. Bake in a preheated oven, 200°C/400°F/Gas Mark 6, for 12–15 minutes, or until the pastry no longer looks raw. Remove the beans and foil and bake for 10 minutes more, or until the pastry is firm, then remove and let cool. Reduce the oven temperature to 180°C/350°F/Gas Mark 4.

2 To make the filling, place the chocolate and butter in a heatproof bowl and melt over a saucepan of gently simmering water. Stir until smooth, then remove from the heat and cool. Place the sugar, flour, vanilla essence and eggs in a separate bowl and whisk until well blended. Stir in the butter and chocolate mixture.

3 Pour the filling into the pastry case and bake in the oven for 50 minutes, or until the filling is just set. Transfer to a wire rack to cool completely. Dust with icing sugar before serving with whipped cream sprinkled lightly with cinnamon.

spiced baked goat's yogurt

ingredients

SERVES 4

200 ml/7 fl oz goat's yogurt

$^1/_4$ tsp ground mixed spice

1 tsp maple syrup

$^1/_4$ tsp vanilla essence

15 g/$^1/_2$ oz dried figs, very finely chopped

1 medium egg white

2 sliced fresh figs, $^1/_4$ tsp maple syrup and fresh mint leaves, to decorate

method

1 Mix the yogurt, mixed spice, maple syrup, vanilla essence and dried figs together in a large bowl.

2 In a separate, very clean, greasefree bowl, lightly whisk the egg white until soft peaks form. Using a metal spoon, fold into the yogurt mixture. Spoon into 4 ramekins or a shallow, ovenproof dish.

3 Stand the ramekins or dish in a roasting pan and half-fill the pan with boiling water. Bake in a preheated oven, 140°C/275°F/Gas Mark 1, for 15 minutes or until set.

4 Remove from the oven. To serve, lay the fresh fig slices on top of the set yogurts, drizzle with maple syrup and decorate with fresh mint leaves.